AT LEFT BRAIN TURN RIGHT

An Uncommon Path to Shutting Up Your
Inner Critic, Giving Fear the Finger
and Having an Amazing Life

Anthony Meindl

At Left Brain Turn Right: An Uncommon Path to Shutting Up Your Inner Critic, Giving Fear the Finger and Having an Amazing Life

Published by:
Meta Creative
7801 Melrose Ave #6, Los Angeles, CA 90046
www.AtLeftBrainTurnRight.com

ISBN: 978-0615534862
ISBN: 0615534864

Printed in the United States of America

"As both a Vipassana meditator and former student of Sanford Meisner himself, I am excited and inspired by Anthony Meindl's synthesis of spiritual awareness and the art of real acting... you will find yourself enriched, both as an artist and - more importantly - as a human being."
Duane Clark, director of CSI: Miami, CSI: New York, Hawaii Five-O

"Tony emphasizes the importance and the TRUTH of living in the moment!"
Trevor Donovan, star of 90210, Savages (dir. Oliver Stone)

"Tony's book is a provocative, thought-provoking new look at the art of acting and what it means to be an artist in the 21st century. It's time for the acting world to re-examine new possibilities for the art form that are set forth by Mr. Meindl."
Jason Clodfelter, VP of Drama Development, Sony Television

"Tony helps actors find the truth within each moment, as they would live it, as they would be in it – without all the unnecessary acting. He encourages the organic, the ability to inhabit a character from within rather than from an artificial place of supposition. And this is where true character is born, where big fat contracts are won. Listen to Tony. He makes good actors."
Abraham Higginbotham, Humanitas Prize Winner and Emmy-Award winning writer of Ugly Betty, Modern Family, producer of Will & Grace

"Tony possesses a passion for and dedication to the craft of acting."
Michael Sucsy, Emmy Award-winning writer/director/producer of HBO's Grey Gardens, director/producer of The Vow

ACKNOWLEDGMENTS

A very special thanks to all the people who helped in this creative undertaking:

To Eric and Robin for shooting down what I thought were a number of great ideas – and thereby sparing me untold amounts of embarrassment. Thank you.

To Nikola … for really doing the same. And always telling me the Truth. Even when it hurts.

To my brother, Chris, who took out the red pen early on in the process. And to my sister, Angie, for lending her wonderful self to some great stories and being willing to look like a "high school hussy" for the sake of art. Now that's commitment!

To my mom and dad just because.

To Olympia Dukakis for her inspiration and constant encouragement to keep exploring deeper truth.

To Christina for keeping me honest. To Nancy, Brian, Sara Anne and Marisa for helping me realize this book had a wider audience.

To Randy and Sam for their amazing artwork. And for Sharon and Barbara for their incredibly insightful editorial eyes.

To all the students I have had the privilege of teaching. Our work together has created this book. Thank you for your inspiration and bravery.

To all the teachers at the studio who continue to spread this unique message in their own beautiful and personal ways: Lindsay, Jonathan, Sean, Emily, Cherry & Christina.

To those artists who've entrusted in me – and explored with me – on this journey virtually from the very beginning. Without you, I would not have an acting studio: Rachel Morgan-Cervantes, Faye Jackson, Coronado Romero, Andrea Davis, Danielle Hoover and Lindsay Frame.

To Paramahansa Yogananda. Whose Light shows me the way. Always.

TABLE OF CONTENTS

AN INTRODUCTION

*"Every child is an artist. The problem is how to
remain an artist once we grow up."*
— Pablo Picasso

We are *all* artists. Every single one of us. From the belly dancer to the banker. From the salesman to the singer. There are as many different ideas about why we are here on this planet as there are people. But what if it's as simple as this: we are all here to *create*.

Authentically. Non-judgmentally. Joyfully. Fearlessly.

The question is — are you?

Are you heeding the call of your true artistic self? Are you willing to do what it takes to silence the inner critic — that fear-based voice that will keep you from manifesting your potential and devise lots of rational-sounding excuses that put your *real* life on hold?

We're all artists, regardless of whether we get paid or not to make art. Whether someone tells us "it's good" and gives us an award, or no one ever notices. Your *life* is your work of art. *You* are the art. And it's more than the sum total of the jobs you book, the paintings you create, the poetry you write, the money you save, the sales you make. It's your joy and hope and love and passion expressed onto this gigantic canvas called Existence. It's been said (and it's true): we are each — individually — the Michelangelo *and* the David of our lives.

But how do we become more conscious of what we're creating and learn to express our creative selves fully in our daily lives? How do we reach the feeling of joy that is our birthright? How do we become liberated from our fears that imprison us? These are our real life goals. As creators. As human beings. And that's a bigger calling than simply being an actor or a lawyer. A musician or a teacher. A painter or a nurse. Yet, wonderfully, our entire lives can be transformed by meeting face-to-face our own potential creative genius. And when we do, we become our own best teacher. Our own best lawyer. Our own best painter or nurse. And isn't that what we're all after? To be our best selves?

So how do we do it? A book agent once asked me why I was specifically qualified to write about creativity.

My answer: Duh. Because I've suffered.

Not the kind of epic suffering that torments millions of people every year. No famine. No civil war. No incurable disease or living below-the-poverty-line. My suffering seemed to be more specific to living in America – a culture that allowed me to have it all and yet something was still missing. How could that be? I had everything and yet still felt as if a part of me needed to be filled. (And actually, the word "suffering" isn't the right word when compared to *real* suffering.) Let's call it unhappiness. A general malaise that strikes so many of us. Boredom. Restlessness. Low-level edginess. Dissatisfaction. Chronic complaining.

Sound familiar?

I was so dramatic. On stage. And off. I wanted out of this feeling. But how?

I started searching. Hard.

I went to India three times. I bathed in the Ganges. (My Indian friends thought I was nuts.) I did weeklong yoga retreats meditating 12 hours a day, not speaking for 10 days straight. "Austerity is the way to enlightenment," I thought. I read books (like the ones in college that made me fall asleep) about every religion known to man and explored the great spiritual truths taught by many teachers. I fed the homeless. I had lots of sex (were the answers hidden there?) and became a work-a-holic. I tried therapy and quitting acting. I found a Guru (or did he find me?) and fasted for days. I did hallucinogens only to be found deep in the forests of Brazil ("Is that lizard talking to me?") and went through a period of celibacy. I went to self-help seminars and workshops and weekend conferences. I wrote pages and pages in my personal diaries, partied, made vision boards and moved cross-country.

Finally, exhausted from all my trying, I screamed to the universe, "I need answers!" Actually, it was something less articulate like, "What the *F***?*"

And then I had an epiphany. Of sorts.

I stopped searching. Instead, I began to live the questions. (Well, not at first. And more like stumbling around in the dark to find the light switch, but hey, I tried.)

Giving up control? Not so easy. But I loosened my demand that the answers had to be given to me in the way I wanted. I realized that the answers I was seeking were there all along. I just didn't want to look. Or sometimes I was truly unable to receive them at the time because I wasn't open to what they wanted to teach me. Ironic, huh? Considering I am a teacher.

I learned that life's potential lies in the *not knowing*: the excitement and fear of throwing yourself into something with abandon — risking embarrassment, failure and ridicule rather than sitting on the sidelines of life asking for a guarantee *before* you take the leap.

I discovered that every time I avoided something, I was, in reality, trying to run away from it.

Actually, I was trying to run away from myself.

The answers I sought were not *out there*. They weren't in a lover or a job or a drug or a TV show or a vacation or a better body or bigger house or nicer car or a reality show or a pay raise or a newborn baby or a marriage or botox or a nose job or even . . . in an acting teacher.

The answers we seek lie within ourselves. Within each of us.

We're all here to learn how to be the creators we truly are. Or, more accurately, to *remember* who we already are. This happens by sharing ourselves — all parts. Even the parts we want to keep hidden. Especially them. The ones we judge most harshly — the icky, scary, ugly ones.

And once we do, the stuff that held us back from our brilliance — our light — becomes the very stuff that is our source of creativity and inspiration.

So that's where our journey begins.

A lot of what's going to help us is to understand the practical applications of many of the concepts I discuss in this book. In order to do so, I use a lot of examples from the work I do with actors.

Why Acting?

Why do you think? Look around. We're everywhere. Our culture is driven by anyone who can become famous for *any reason*, using their popularity to sell products. A lot of times, it's actors. Other times it's an athlete who takes on celebrity status or a YouTube star who brands himself. But the truth is, we *all* act. Some of us just get paid a lot of money to do it. Acting — perhaps more than any other art form and any other profession — can be understood as a metaphor to make points about who we are — and aren't — as people.

It seems we're living in a time where we relate to each other not through who we are but through the roles we play — which include what we accomplish, how much money we make, how we look on Facebook, how famous or beautiful we are, how many hits we get on YouTube and how clever we tweet. Our culture is so oriented toward the roles people play and how we *appear* to others that when someone shatters those illusions — either negatively or positively — we're often left having to deconstruct the myths we believed about them in the first place.

Celebrity is our national obsession. Our desire for our 15 minutes of fame (at any cost) illustrates how we're all actors, whether we're famous or not. Our interest in actors partly has to do with our culture's elimination of archetypes. American society has no archetypes to draw from in order to forge more authentic lives. Historically, most cultures have created through Divine archetypes to help human beings realize their innate potential and connect to nature and something greater than their personas. The ancient Greeks would utilize the pantheon of gods and goddesses, Native Americans created totemic rituals, and today, much of India relies on Hindu gods and goddesses to help them personify qualities they wish to evoke within themselves. Americans have no ancient mythological archetypal models to inspire us.

One could argue that we do, but almost all of them are derived not from nature or spirit or some other existential quality, but ironically through TV and film images and celebrity itself. There's Cinderella (the rags-to-riches story), June & Wally Cleaver ("family values"), and the underdog hero who "makes it" – Rocky Balboa.

Because the identification with mythology is hard-wired within us as a people, we're going to search. And since media of every type and the use of social networking sites are becoming *the form* of storytelling in our culture, our new role models have become celebrities born of this technology. Not because they inspire something within us but simply because they're on TV. So, *The Apprentice's* Omarosa takes the place of Medusa. A famous celebrity being thrown into jail for numerous infractions fulfills our need to see the fall of the tragic hero. Contemporary Schadenfreude.

But the question remains. Are reality stars who become famous for eating cockroaches or beating each other up while on vacation in Italy fulfilling the deeper desire within each of us to connect to our own archetypes to realize our potential?

Our fascination with actors comes from what psychologists say is our over-exposure to celebrity-infused media; causing us to invite actors into our homes through the media we receive. They inhabit our universe and we enact certain roles learned by watching them. They become our extended family. Even if we've never met them. If we follow their tweets, we're a part of their lives.

We dress like them, mimic them, parody them, read about them, have websites built for them, talk like them, demand answers from them, tweet with them, Facebook friend-request them, stalk them, deify them, vilify them, make fun of them, and want to be them. They become our role models, our heroes, our disappointments, our cultural scapegoats, our surrogate parents. We buy their records and DVDs, their perfumes and make-up and nail polish and hair products, their jeans and shoes and handbags and sunglasses, their books and movies, their work-out programs and cookware and skin care packages and fashion lines.

Actors (and celebrities of any kind) in short, *are* our culture. But what if they – and you (and all of us!) – are so much more than the roles we assume? What if transcending our self-ascribed labels, definitions and judgments led us to an entirely new relationship with ourselves? What if everything we ever needed is deeply buried within ourselves and the journey is a journey inward. Not outward. But in order to access it we first have to know we possess it. And we also have to identify the fears that hold us back. That's not always easy, because just like the acting masks we wear on a daily basis that keep us hidden from the world, fear hides itself through many different faces: resistance, doubt, impatience, judgment, sarcasm, negativity, complaining, comparing, procrastination, avoidance, pessimism, denial and cynicism are just a few. I dabble in all of them on a daily basis. *Rats!* The goal is to first become aware of them. Then we can dismantle them. We'll do that in this book.

We're also going to cover a lot of other ground here. There are homework exercises (one lesson a week for the next 15 weeks) that might help you discover creative worlds you never knew existed. Think of it as a workbook to be used any way you like.

The next 15 weeks may be asking you to suspend your conditioned thinking. You know, that voice that's the first to tell you something isn't possible. Don't believe it. It's been keeping you in the dark too long. It's time to unlock access to your right brain and let as much light in as you can. Try stepping into a new way of thinking. It may question old-view paradigms you've outgrown — and ask you to create a new framework from which to see yourself, and what's possible. Isn't that exciting? Couldn't it be fun? Our built-in biases will still be there to reclaim after the experiment if you choose to re-adopt them. I'm hoping you won't.

So really the question to ask yourself is, "What do I have to lose?"

WHO DO YOU THINK YOU ARE?

"For me there is only the traveling on paths that have heart. On any path that may have heart, there I travel. And the only worthwhile challenge is to traverse its full length. And there I travel looking, looking breathlessly."
— Carlos Castaneda

We're not our stuff. The jobs or the money we have. The cars we drive. The houses we own. The women or men we date. The titles we acquire. The awards we've won. The fortunes we've amassed. Or the year we were born.

So if we aren't these things, who are we? When was the last time we asked, "Why am I here? What's life really about? Who am I?"

The first step in the journey is to uncover who we *aren't.*

Who we are has nothing to do with age or sex or hair color. It has no concern for whether we're a size two or thirty pounds overweight. It just wants to be expressed. Actually, it doesn't even want that. It just *is*. It's the part of us concealed by the ramblings and rantings of our super-sized egos trying to run the show.

Our essence — our *being* — has been waiting patiently for us to discover that it's been there all along. Sadly, we become so identified with our external trappings, we lose connection to our deeper nature. We're so invested in what we do, what we wear, who we know, how we look, where we live, what we achieve, and what others say about us, that we become dependent upon these outer identifications for our self-worth. We relate to the outer more than the inner.

"Be" is a verb, giving rise to the pronoun "am." Instead of saying, "I be," we say, "I am." But it means the same thing: "I am *being*." In other words, I *am* something before I *do* anything. That "something" transcends being man or woman, black or white, a janitor or a CEO, or any other number of ways we're defined.

The more we identify with the external, the more we lose the sense of real connection with ourselves and with other human beings. Spiritually and scientifically, we're all connected. That connection transcends whether we were born in Indiana or Iceland.

As artists — which is who we all are —we have a calling to connect with our deepest, authentic selves. Creativity allows us to experience that part of ourselves that *is* the artistry. But how do we take the deep connection and understanding that accompanies creativity out into the world without limiting it to our art?

In other words, how do we become more conscious of creating? Always and in all ways? Not just in our chosen profession?

Drum roll, please: Stop judging yourself.

> *"Out beyond ideas of wrong doing and right doing, there is a field. I'll meet you there."*
> — Jalalud'din Rumi, *13th-century mystic poet*

At one level, Rumi's talking about greeting all people, all situations without judgment. Without ego arrogance that says one opinion is better or more correct than another. At a deeper level, he's beckoning us to join him at the Quantum Field. Einstein's Unified Field posits that our being (and all things) originate from a field from which all fundamental forces are derived. It's the ground of the universe where *all* things emerge.

Connection.

In science, the basic structure of everything is the atom. And at its core level, the atom is vibrating energy: the basic building block of all matter in the physical world. That's what we are. Pulsating, dynamic and constantly transforming energy. And energy is simply raw potential. That's our essence. That's our *being*. Pure potential. That's who we are.

Your Being In Relation To Your Art

When I tell my acting students that their being — who we all are — is quantum energy; that energy can neither be created nor destroyed, and their real work is to start becoming aware of themselves at an energetic level, they stare blankly. I know what they're thinking: "Is this a science class?" "When do I get to pretend to be a monkey?" "I just want to be on *America's Next Top Model*." "Ummmm…I enrolled in class to bang hot chicks."

We've been inundated with so many misleading theories about creating that we think if we aren't working hard to "get it," or struggling through the process, then we must not be learning. What would happen if we just let go of the struggle?

When we were kids, our ability to play, create and imagine was probably (until it got screwed-up by grown-ups who didn't know any better), a *joyful* experience. It was easy. Somewhere along the way we began making something that comes naturally to us — difficult.

Why? Because we love the drama.

Plato believed education wasn't a process of putting knowledge into empty minds, but of realizing what is already known. "You mean a deeper part of me already knows this stuff and I've just spent a fortune listening to some 'expert' tell me what I thought only he knew?" Yep. Pretty much. Smart marketing. And one way to keep us coming back again and again, spending more time and money relinquishing our power and inner knowing to someone we *perceive* as having all the answers or the key to happiness or the way to make a fortune or the way to become famous.

You have the answers.

"But Tony, how do we find it, damn it?" Well, we need to stop looking *out there*.

Will The Real Teacher Please Stand Up?

My parents didn't teach me how to be (although they were and continue to be wonderful parents). The educational system didn't teach me (I was too busy trying to become a straight-A student, getting away from being by achieving). Many of my acting teachers didn't. They taught me the *doing*: stressing goals, objectives, intentions. So where did I learn how to be? (And by no stretch of the imagination do I have this process mastered.) Actually, I knew it all the time, as we all do. But over the course of a lifetime, I unlearned it. I grew up listening to what other people thought was best for me, doing all the things I was "supposed" to do, and I forgot who I was.

It may seem obvious that we *are,* but surprisingly, many of us don't know how to be with ourselves, or with our feelings, or with others in a conscious way. We're taught very early that life is about success; measured by our achievements, the things we do, the things we accumulate.

To avoid who we are, we run away from what we feel. We distract ourselves, constantly trying to remain stimulated. Sometimes we binge on booze, food, cigarettes, sex, shopping or drugs. Other times we obsess and worry and make phone calls and gossip, watch TV and text and instant message, tweet and Facebook and google, shoot video and update social network statuses, run on the treadmill, shop, download and e-date while reading *People* magazine and channel-surfing through 587 choices. All in the span of 10 minutes.

Multi-tasking in the new millennium. Without consciousness. We're not present (but fool ourselves into thinking we are). We're "connected" but lack connection. We're dreaming, wishing for a new tomorrow, thinking life is better elsewhere. Anywhere. But it's not. It's right here. Right now. Only we're so driven by distractions, we constantly miss it.

A.D.D. America

We're obsessed with the climax. The end result. But what about the foreplay? We're rewarded for doing a million things at once, no matter how *not* present we are while doing them, as long as the tasks get done. This non-mindfulness erodes our ability to be present with people in a meaningful way. Think about it. When was the last time you actually had a conversation with someone while *not* looking at your Blackberry or tweeting your location or checking your iPhone for the latest NFL score at the same time? How often have you been talking with your boss while sex-ting your booty-call?

How many times are we made to feel that if we don't have what everyone else has or be a part of the newest fad or watch the hottest show or be invited to the "in" party, we're missing out or we're going to be left behind in some way? That our lives are incomplete?

Ugh. It's high school all over again. It never ends.

Why is society constantly trying to fill us? Is it because many of us "have everything" and still feel empty, having lost the connection with the greater part of ourselves? Or maybe we haven't been taught what the greater part of ourselves is?

Since none of these outer things can ever satiate us, our culture keeps coming up with new ways to try. More gadgets, more toys and adult playthings, more websites, more shocking stories, more TV teasers, more gossip that can only be revealed if we "tune in at 11."

"Oh, no. What am I going to miss if I don't tune in?" Nothing.

Madonna's "American Life" says it all.

I'm drinkin' a soy latte
I get a double shoté
It goes right through my body
And you know I'm satisfied
I do yoga and pilates
And the room is full of hotties
So I'm checking out their bodies
And you know I'm satisfied
I'm diggin' on the isotope
This metaphysics shit is dope
And if all this can give me hope
You know I'm satisfied

I got a lawyer and a manager
An agent and a chef
Three nannies, an assistant
And a driver and a jet
A trainer and a butler
And a bodyguard or five
A gardener and a stylist
Do you think I'm satisfied?

Sociologist and researcher Dr. Brené Brown reports that, "we are the most in-debt, obese, addicted, and medicated adult cohort in U.S. history." Eeeeeek. Why? Because what we're grasping for — what we're searching for — that we mistakenly think is in all these things *out there,* is actually the deeper connection to Self.

So the question is, "Are you satisfied" with who you are? Not with what you accumulate or amass or collect or purchase or achieve?

I'm not saying we should all be Buddhist monks and have a garage sale of all our earthly possessions. Enjoy the fruits of your labors — whether it's a million dollars or a soy latte — you've earned it. I mean, look at Madonna. Hello. But when our actions come from a purer place of being, we have a more conscious, present, awakened and full life. Full from within.

"We are so engaged in doing things to achieve purposes of outer value that we forget that the inner value, the rapture that is associated with being alive, is what it's all about."
— **Joseph Campbell,** *scholar*

Whether you're a poet or carpenter, a teacher or a singer, our journeys are about unlearning a great deal of what we've already been "taught" so we can then re-learn how to do it *our way*. Teaching actors is an interesting example of this because, for generations, it's been taught as the art and process of "doing," of going after one's goals, of taking action. Teachers have been training students from the presupposition that actors know how to be. News flash: we don't. Very few people know how to *be* in this world. First, because few people are teaching us. And second, we're taught from an early age to *do*. "What do I want, and how am I going to get it?" is the great battle cry of Americans.

Being Precedes Action — In Life And In Creating

Once we become present to each moment in life we have to acknowledge our feelings. We don't want to feel, so we push out, we act, we do, we show. In extreme cases, that ends up as compulsions and addictions — tuning out in some way— so that feelings can be kept at bay. Sometimes when I reach for that bag of Oreo cookies, it's because I'm freaked out by situations that give rise to uncomfortable feelings. Instead of feeling them, I shove them down by stuffing my face. Or gossiping. Or talking on the phone about nothing. Or exercising compulsively. Or smoking. Or having a few beers. Or surfing the internet for porn. Or scoring a deal on Amazon.

Avoidance takes many forms.

When the devastating tsunami battered large parts of Japan in 2011, the images and stories that we encountered were haunting. One day my friend, John, called and screamed, "Turn on CNN!" I did and was moved to tears by the tsunami victims' accounts of what they endured. I called John back. "Intense, huh?" In a panic he mumbled, "I have to hang up." "Why," I asked. "The pain's too much. I have to go eat a bowl of cereal." Click.

Gulping down a bowl of Count Chocula can temporarily drown the pain. It's chocolaty, tasty goodness. When I called John back, he joked that it had indeed done the trick. This is what we do in life. We don't want to feel. So we tune out in any way possible to avoid. My go-to cereal is Cap'n Crunch. With Crunch-berries.

Don't despair. There are ways to become aware when we're tuning out, and to use this awareness as an opportunity to tune in. By tuning in, we tap into the emotional and creative potential we each possess. We can heal and reshape our lives. We can actually live the lives we always intended for ourselves.

One way we tune out — and may not even realize it — is through our constant use of, and being distracted by, our "personal media devices." Remember when they were just called phones?

This first week of homework is all about how we use "things" to check out. Specifically, our phones. Maybe the easiest way to get started is to confront something that we've become so dependent on (and everyone uses) that we probably have an addiction to — and aren't even aware.

Homework, Week 1: For one week, turn the phones off. Are you getting nervous at just the thought? Are your palms getting sweaty? Welcome to our new cultural addiction. Don't freak out. We're just at week one. I'm not saying you can't use the phone at all for an entire week. Instead, try limiting its use.

This week, don't answer your phone while having a lunch meeting, or while you're with someone else. Don't text someone while in the middle of a face-to-face conversation with another person. Don't check it every 10 minutes. Don't take it to bed with you and leave it on so you can get hourly tweet updates. The information you think is so important and must be answered immediately — I promise you — can wait an hour. Or a full day.

Observe how often you reach for the device out of habit. How often you try to keep busy and distracted by playing with the phone rather than just being. How many times have you pretended to be on the phone when you went to a crowded function? Or pretended to be texting someone or responding to an email? Be honest. We do this out of our insecurity. We are so not in our bodies that we make up things to keep us on the constant wheel of doing.

What would happen if the next time you were waiting for someone (a date, perhaps?) to arrive at a public place (the movies or a restaurant or a coffee shop) you simply waited for them? Don't download an iTunes App, don't play *Angry Birds*, don't search through old emails. Just be. See what you discover. Record your thoughts if you want. But try it. For one week.

When you normally reach for your cell phone to distract you or to make you feel more important or re-assured or in control — how about reaching for a breath instead. Just take a deep, cleansing breath. And again. And again. And as you do, you've just had an experience of your being. See how simple it is when we aren't distracted?

(After each homework exercise, there is a blank page to record your thoughts. To write down something that came to you as an inspiration, an idea, an epiphany. Use it as a diary. Use it to check in on how you are progressing with the homework. Use it as a place to allow your creative self to be expressed. Use it however you wish.)

"Your time is limited, so don't waste it living someone else's life. Don't be trapped by dogma - which is living with the results of other people's thinking. Don't let the noise of other's opinions drown out your own inner voice. And most important, have the courage to follow your heart and intuition. They somehow already know what you truly want to become. Everything else is secondary."

— Steve Jobs

LISTEN UP, PEOPLE!

"Listen. Do not have an opinion while you listen,
because frankly, your opinion doesn't hold much
water outside of your universe. Just listen. Listen
until their brain has been twisted like a dripping
towel and what they have to say is all over the floor."
— Hugh Elliott

I'm single. It is what it is. Maybe one of the reasons I *am* single is that I keep having to relearn that whenever I go out on a date, it always goes much better when I keep my mouth shut and let the date do the talking. Partly because I reveal too much. But also, if I let them talk, they tell me who they are.

Just listen.

Every time I've gotten into trouble in life, had I kept my mouth shut, I probably wouldn't be in the drama that's now causing so much stress.

Just listen.

People tell us what we really need to hear. Sadly, we miss most of it — and often at our own detriment — because we can't do this one little thing.

Listening — not talking — is really a state of being. I'm not simply describing that process which most people ascribe to the organ known as the ear. Listening is actually a person's ability to *be* with another person physically, emotionally, psychologically and spiritually.

It's difficult for us to be with our own feelings, let alone someone else's. So we fill that space with mindless, comforting chatter because of nerves or ego, or trying to control a situation. Feelings, as you may now realize, make us uncomfortable. Then why the hell do we have them? Ironically, to help us learn to *be*.

I Want You To Feel — Just Not Feel *Those* Feelings

Ever notice that instead of truly being with someone, we often impose our prejudices, fears, likes and dislikes onto another? We say things like, "Don't cry," or "Everything will be okay," to a friend who's grieving. Maybe things aren't okay for him right now. Maybe he wants to have a complete emotional breakdown and have someone simply listen.

Yes, sometimes people ask us for our help and want our words of comfort and encouragement. But what if we became aware of how often we fill moments of our listening — our being — with not listening. We feel very uncomfortable that our friend's letting go of his stuff. Maybe it brings up our own buried feelings or anxiety about feeling, and suddenly, instead of sharing our friend's pain by being with him, we fill the void by cracking a joke, or rationalizing the situation, or making the moment about ourselves.

Imagine how uncomfortable it feels to witness someone who is an authority figure, someone who seems to "have it all together," like a mentor or a parent, having an emotional release. We just freak, don't we? It's as if the image of them having real feelings is too scary. It completely destroys the picture we have of them. Like water thrown on an exposed electrical unit, it sparks and explodes.

The Gift That Keeps On Giving

When I was a teen, my dad went through a rough patch in his life. One year at Christmas, he disappeared after a huge blow-out with my mom and my older brother. Poof, he was gone. Very David Blaine Vegas Magic Show. His car was in the garage but he'd vanished. In a panic, my sister, Angie, and I went searching for him. My mom put her frustrations into tenderizing the hell out of the wiener schnitzel we were having for dinner that night and my brother stalked off to his room to play AC/DC records *really* loudly.

Angie and I walked around the house meekly calling out, "Dad?" I looked in the obvious places (his bedroom and bathroom) more than once. Like a child playing hide-and-seek, I retraced my steps thinking I'd somehow overlooked him. Suddenly, my sister called out. She found him sitting in our downstairs basement closet, sobbing. We wouldn't have thought to look in that walk-in closet (it's where all our summer clothes and oversized suitcases were stored and smelled like mothballs), but she heard my dad crying from outside the door.

Angie and I stared at each other, a deer-in-the-headlights look. She tried to console him, while I — showing the flair for the dramatic at an early age — completely lost it. It was as if my internal computer was saying, "This does not compute!" What the hell was dad doing in the walk-in closet where I'd put on private fashion shows for myself wearing the latest JC Penny and Sears summer outfits? When you're a kid you don't recognize parents as human: fallible, messy, struggling with hopes and dreams and major challenges of their own — just like we do now as adults. As kids, we assume they have it all together, right?

At the time, I didn't understand that my dad was just like every other person on the planet and needed to be: with himself, his anger, his sadness, his rage, his disappointment; with everything. He didn't allow himself the freedom to feel in front of us. It makes sense that he sought refuge in a place where his being could just let go without feeling judged. In that closet, he didn't have to keep it together for everyone else.

Now that I'm an adult and have had my own kinds of breakdowns — some public, some private — I see how important it is to be with someone, if they desire, when they're having an emotional release, allowing them to simply have the experience. It's a selfless act to be with another person. Not just during emotional times but always doing the best we can to become more conscious, more present, with the person standing next to us. This is the gift we can give every moment to every person we meet. It can positively alter the relationships we have with others (from our parents to the pharmacist to our next door neighbor).

Can you imagine who we'd become if we learned how to *be* in this selfless way?

You Hear Me But Are You Listening?

When I first learned how to act, I had no idea that the concept of listening was *the* catalyst for transforming my work (and my life). The idea of listening seemed easy. "I listen all the time," I thought to myself. "This can't be all there is to it." I realized, much to my dismay, that I heard things when I had to, but I rarely listened.

Kind of like life. I didn't really listen to what people said. I could hardly wait until they shut up so I could say something more interesting. At the same time, my mind was filled with such noise (judgments, criticisms, fears) it kept me from truly being with another person. Listening wasn't so easy. Because listening meant having to give up control. And who wants to do that?

I remember the first time I actually listened in a scene in a receptive fashion. After the scene was over, I thought, "What just happened?" I couldn't remember any of the specifics. The experience was exhilarating and ended after what seemed like a few seconds, while at the same time, lasted forever.

It was like the most amazing sex ever: transcendent, joyful, ecstatic. (Not sloppy-hooking-up-after-10-beers-I-can't-remember-your-name sex.) The actual listening experience onstage transcended the mental concepts I had of how I thought the scene would play out. I went beyond just hearing enough to get me to what came next in the scene. Rather than trying to cause something to happen, for the first time in my acting, I was actually *surrendering* to the effect. It was timeless.

One of the biggest challenges to becoming present is our insistence on how we think something should look. How many times have you rehearsed in your head the things you wanted to say to someone and how you wanted to say them? How many times have you cleverly planned how you wanted something to turn out? We do this all the time, right? When the actual time comes, however, life has a way of forcing us to respond to what it's giving us, as opposed to holding on to our memorized script.

The last time I got dumped, I thought up a number of extraordinary conversations I would have with my ex if I ever ran into him again. You know the kind. Full of violins playing and tear-stained apologies and running off together. Happy ever after.

Yeah . . . no.

I *did* run into my ex. With his new boyfriend. Ouch. The only articulate thing I said was, "Oh . . . hi!" Then out of sheer panic I vomited, "Do you remember the camera you bought me for Christmas? Well, I was just in Brazil and dropped it in the ocean — actually a huge wave, like, swept it out to sea, but how great I'm running into you again, 'cause if you still have the receipt I'll just return it and get a new one. I mean, it's under warranty. You got it at Best Buy, right?"

O. M. G. Please tell me I did not just say that.

Awkward. He stared. I freaked. I bolted, grabbing my friend who'd accompanied me to the party, locking us in the bathroom for 25 minutes where a complete meltdown ensued.

Life happens to us. Unscripted. What's the saying? Man plans. God laughs.

Mind Trips

Soon after this embarrassing run-in with my ex — I decided to start dating again. (I mean, obviously, he wasn't sitting around pining away for me like I hoped he was.) One day at the gym I saw this hot (I mean, *hawt!*) guy working behind the counter at the juice bar. "Oh my Gawd," I thought, running to my Afro-Brazilian dance class (¡Aye Carumba!) Yes, that's right — Afro-Brazilian. Don't judge. Anyway, I decided that I'd ask the "beauty of smoothies" out on a date when I finished the class an hour later. Love connection.

As I shimmied and shook my way across the sweaty dance floor (take that, Shakira), I thought of all the things I would say to my future husband. I daydreamed every possible permutation of frozen vanilla-protein-powder milkshake love: from an embarrassing refusal, to our getting married as the sun sinks behind us on the beaches of Tahiti, to honeymooning in Paris, to going on a wild

African safari (cue lion's roar here). When I finished with class, I dashed (was I being obvious?) to the juice bar only to see — oh the *horror!* — that the object of my affection, the man I had planned on spending the rest of my life with, had been replaced by a *very hairy* muscle man in tiny blue spandex shorts (OMG. I could read his religion) and an extra-tight, pink, spaghetti-strapped T-shirt obviously bought in the junior section at baby Gap to amplify his artificially enhanced, bulging pectoral muscles. He was a hirsute throwback to Arnold Schwarzenegger in *Conan the Barbarian*. Or a male version of Lucy Lawless circa her *Xena: Warrior Princess* days. I couldn't decide which. Gulp. "Isn't there a dress code here?" I thought to myself. "Anyone this juiced should *not* work at a juice bar."

Sadly, my future dream-husband was gone for the day. But really, during my class, so was I. I wasn't present to the experience of being in class, to my body flying through the air and other dancers laughing and clapping. To my bare feet sliding across the wooden floor and the hypnotic beats of the thumping drums. I might as well not even have attended. I was lost in that no-man's land of the left brain spinning (worst- and best-case) scenarios when I should've been spinning it on the dance floor instead. Work it!

Oh, how our mind-trips always seem more exciting than experiencing real life. That's why we often spend so much time there. Too bad they're illusions. Wake up, and smell the Sanka.

So how the hell do we get out of our heads when we're in them? Listen.

Cause & Effect

In my working with actors I've noticed that the transformative work occurs not in the words an actor speaks, but *first* in their reaction to the words spoken to them. Feelings, thoughts, chemical reactions, and physiological, as well as physical changes occur within us before we speak. Words then represent, symbolize, explain, or reference these feelings. They're a result or effect, not a cause. Sure, I may say something that causes feelings in you, but notice how the feeling or thoughts about what is being said to you come before the articulation of the words you now wish to speak to me in return.

In fact, we often get into trouble in life when we simply react to what we hear and don't allow ourselves to listen at a deeper level. But deep listening is a function of being fully present and of allowing ourselves to be emotionally affected.

How has your *heart* been affected? The purpose of great art (and also the experience one has while creating it) is to touch others. It affects both the person receiving the art (watching it or listening to it or reading it) and the person who's creating it. If our heart isn't affected and it doesn't touch other people at a deep level, then really, why do it? And I might argue, then, that it isn't real art. I mean, one man's trash is another man's treasure, for sure, so it's all subjective. But what *moves* you?

Tony Don't Call Us, We'll Call You

In my first-ever professional job as an actor I got my ass kicked. I had no idea what deep listening was. I was young and cocky (which I later realized was just a compensation for my utter lack of confidence and low self-esteem). I thought I could get by on tricks and a hell of a lot of charm.

Survey says: Wrong.

I was screwed. Every time I said a line, the energy in the room left the building. All heads turned to stare at me. Terror. Was I that bad? First came the puddles-underneath-my-armpits sweat. Then my body temperature rose as if there was a furnace being lit from inside. My palms got clammy. My face turned prickly red. My throat tightened. Cottonmouth. Gross. And terrifying. Every artist, surely, has felt this response at some point in life.

After a rehearsal, the famous Tony Award-winning director marched toward me across a long stage. (Actually, he was less a director and more dictator — yelling and screaming at me constantly — but at the tender age of 23 I thought he was God. He'd directed on Broadway, after all, so I subjugated myself at the feet of Herr Abuser.) The echoes of his clomping foot-steps reverberated in my head. "Is he wearing clogs? Crocs? Birkenstocks? How very 'Island of Lesbos' of him," I thought. I braced for impact. "Charm him, Tony. Play dumb."

He leaned into my face; his hot breath smelled of coffee and stale cigarettes – the diet of directors in those days. This was not going to be pretty. The other cast-mates gawked, frozen in silence. He stared for what seemed an interminable amount of time. I felt my bowels rumble. Pooping my pants felt imminent. Oh, Lord. I knew I was about to be shamed. There's nothing worse than the terror and humiliation an actor faces within him-self when confronted with the brutal fact that he might be the worst actor ever to step on any stage. Anywhere.

"Tony," he whispered, which seemed unnecessary because everyone was already stone-cold silent. "You're acting. Stop. Doing. That. Right. Now."

Huh? Total panic. I didn't know how to do anything else but "act." Holy shit. How can you know there's something *other* if you didn't know you were doing something *else* in the first place?

My eyes welled with tears and I ran crying out of the room all the way to my hotel. (Can you say Drama Empress?) I called five different airlines to book the next available flight out of Pittsburgh. (Sienna Miller called it "Shittsburgh" but terrible rehearsal experience, notwithstanding, I loved it.) "Why should I stay here though and be ridiculed," I panicked. "If I'm not even aware that I'm doing something that I shouldn't be doing? Stop acting? What the hell does he mean? I'm not acting."

Through some sort of divine intercession, my parents called while an airline had me on hold for what seemed like forever, subjecting me to the repeated playback loop of the instrumental version of *We Are The World*, sending my already-frayed nerves into an emotional breakdown. (Did I mention I had a flair for the dramatic?) I clicked over, screaming, "I've been on hold for 15 minutes. I can't talk right now. I'm coming home. I can't do this. I quit!" My mom replied calmly, "Whatever you decide is fine by us. But maybe you should just try your best. He did hire you, after all."

Ding. Light bulb moment. Try my best, huh? Kind of hard for a self-described perfectionist. But it made sense. And she was right. He hired my lame ass. Shouldn't he have known better? Broadway director, indeed.

With a new resolve and a sort of perverse pleasure in seeing him squirm as he watched me "act," I decided I could endure. For my art.

But at the time I had no idea that acting came from my listening under the given circumstances of the play as *me* first. Holy crap, I wasn't even in the theatre. I was literally, but figuratively I was trying to play this "character" as someone else (a young Tom Cruise circa *Risky Business*, let's say, when he was way cool). I'd go to the lines and say them as the director wanted and how I thought they'd sound if "Tommy" said them. I was a robot. Can you imagine? Now I know why the director hated me.

I muddled through the rehearsals in a constant state of anxiety. The increasingly close-to-having-an-apoplectic-seizure director wanted me to be more sexual, more playful, more flirtatious; all these things that I could do in my real life if I was on a date and

I wanted to get laid. But in this play, without my listening first to what my scene partner was telling me — which would naturally change the way I would say a line — I tried going to the text first and then add sexuality on top of each line. Talk about schizophrenia. I was trying to be Mr. Cruise *trying* to be this character *trying* to say these lines the way I thought someone should sound who is playful or sexy. Tragic. And definitely not sexy.

Well how the hell should I've known? I'd never been taught that my essential being had to first be available to act without falsity. (And now that I think about it, the director didn't know either, because he'd have told me.) Years later, working with thousands of actors, I still notice many are not being given this foundation — the building block — for everything else in their work. They haven't learned that it can only come from listening.

My reviews, by the way, were horrible. But what I love about recalling them now — and didn't understand then — is they commented on this very thing I've been talking about. They said I, "merely said the lines without any meaning behind them." Well, duh. There was no meaning because I wasn't listening.

If It Were So Easy Everyone Would Be Doing It

But it's not and people aren't.

"Talking and listening . . . to do that is the beginning and end of acting for me and it's not as easy as it looks sometimes. Everyone says, 'Oh, you're just yourself up there.' And I say, try it. Try it. It's not that easy."
— Robert Duvall, *Academy Award winner*

Go and watch actors sometime. A lot of "acting" is going on but hardly any listening. Sometimes, this art of listening is so rarely executed that when an actor does listen onstage, it's a watershed moment.

Ben Brantley in his 2010 *New York Times* review of the play, *A Lie of the Mind,* wrote, "the cast members deliver these lines as if they had either just thought of them or had been saying them all their lives." I thought, "Really Ben? This is the way it's supposed to be." But we so seldom see it, that when it happens, it is electric. If more actors were taught how to listen, this kind of commentary would be the rule, not the exception.

By activating real listening, we lose the control of saying a line the way we think it should sound, or how we've rehearsed it, or how we think the character should say it. Instead, we're forced to work with how listening to the words being said makes us feel. In life and in acting. Active listening moves us from living our lives in a safe, vacuum-like dress rehearsal — full of control, planning, and familiarity — into the power of the moment. It's like moving from the grey monochromatic movie of our dull lives into vibrant, unpredictable Technicolor.

Hearing each word is not going to make us listen any better. Words are actively sent and felt with content and meaning. We listen to the intent of words. For example, we respond to what a person doesn't say, as much as to what is said, and how the person says it. You've been dating someone for a few months, and one night your steady says, "I like you." We think, "Well, what does that mean? Is she in love with me? Does she just want to be friends? Is she trying to be nice because she's going to dump me? Is she going to ask me to meet her parents?" We then send words back based on how we've perceived and interpreted her message.

Do We Say What We Mean Or Mean What We Say?

Sometimes we create meaning in what was said to us that's totally unrelated to the intended meaning. We misperceive and misinterpret. My brother asks me, "Tony, did you get your haircut?" I don't just hear, "Did you get a haircut?" I hear, "Tony you got your hair cut and ummm . . . you might want to reconsider it." Or when someone says, "I can't hang out with you tomorrow," we hear, "I don't like you anymore," or "I'm losing interest." The person may just mean "I can't hang out with you tomorrow," but we add our own psychological or emotional meaning to the words. Be honest. Haven't you done this a thousand times?

My friend, Diane, called me recently, ranting about her boyfriend who called her, "an Amazon." Hysterical, she hung up on him, calling me immediately. "Stewart called me an Amazon!" "Uh-huh," I responded. "What does that mean?" she moaned. I stalled. Partly because I didn't know. But I knew enough to know calling Diane an Amazon wasn't a good thing. It could mean a bad-ass warrior goddess or long-legged beauty queen. But knowing Diane, I knew that *that* was not how she heard it.

Her mind spun out of control. "Is he saying I'm big-boned? Or too tall? Or gigantic . . . am I fat? Aren't Amazonians like gigantic she-men living in a jungle? Is he calling me a he-she? OMG. I'm a fat he-she!" she screamed. Since we make up our own meaning to the things that are often said to us, and out of our neuroses generally choose the most awful explanation, she opted for what she felt was the worst possible definition for her.

Of course he didn't say she was a "fat he-she" (I'm still not even sure what that is), but in her mind he did. And it was over. She broke up with the poor schmuck the next day. That's why it's always important to have someone listen for you in times of intense emotional arguments with your significant other, if you don't want to risk the eventual doom of a disastrous break-up. Our listening is all we have, but it will always be filtered through our own expectations, dreams, opinions, likes and dislikes, agendas and fears.

My assistant said something recently in answer to a question I had asked her. When she spoke, I wasn't paying attention. I was somewhere in my head thinking about something else I had to do later that day. Later is later. Now is now. If I am fully present to now the later will take care of itself. I had to ask her to repeat what she said. Twice.

Next time, just listen.

Homework, Week 2: Take five minutes at the beginning and end of each day for one week, and simply sit, close your eyes, and breathe. Thoughts will come and go. Observe them as best you can, as a witness of something un-extraordinary. Simply try to let go of your association with all the things you have done for the day and be with your breath. As you're able to go deeper with sitting in this stillness — either in duration or depth — become aware of an association or feeling of something within yourself that is your Self and yet isn't the little ego self you've been spending years trying to build. Sit in silence for as long as you can (but at least five minutes a day) every day for one week.

There are many ways to sit in silence. One way is to count your breath by inhaling for an eight-count and then exhaling on an eight-count. (Or you could do shorter counts.

Whatever feels most comfortable.) You could light a candle and simply watch the flickering flame, letting it take you into a deeper and more peaceful state. You could repeat a mantra, like, "I am peace. I am joy. I am light," over and over again. You could close your eyes and scan your body, becoming aware of where you're holding tension and where you're in pain. As you recognize those areas, you can breathe into those places to release the body.

You can find Sanskrit or Buddhist texts and repeat the holy words. You could close your eyes and pray deeply to whatever Deity feels right to pray to, and after you have emptied your heart, sit in the silence and emptiness. You can evoke one of the more than hundred ways to say God and repeat it over and over again. If "God" isn't your cup of tea, you can simply sit and express gratitude for all the things you have in your life. If you're having a hard time finding anything to be grateful for, you can sit, close your eyes, and contemplate an idea or image that comes to mind. Maybe it's a scenic location you love going to. Maybe it's a new explanation for something you wish to ponder further. If you're feeling vocal, you can sing a hymn or prayerful song. Sing it loudly and repeatedly, and as you continue, get quieter and quieter until you begin to sing it silently to yourself. You can visualize yourself (and everything on this planet) in a white ball of light and then let that ball soar freely into the cosmos. You get the idea?

When teaching meditation, I think it's important for the practitioner to discover the method that works best for him, so I often just suggest a few general ways of sitting in silence. I don't want the way I do something to influence your own discovery and process. I truly believe your body will tell you what's best. So sit in the chair or get in a yoga pose or lie down and see what you discover. Sometimes, people will tell me, "Oh, Tony, I can't quiet my mind." Or, "I can't stop my thoughts." These are ultimately excuses to keep you from sitting in the meditation chair and doing your work. The goal is not to end thought — that's impossible as long as we are in this physical body. Don't give yourself an impossible task. Be gentle with yourself. The act of committing to a meditation practice will show you what you need to know. But you have to take the first step.

I can tell you one thing for certain. If you commit to this, you will never regret having tried meditating. Ever. So what do you have to lose?

"There is nothing in a caterpillar that tells you it's going to be a butterfly."
— Buckminster Fuller

THE MAN WITH TWO BRAINS

"Sit down before fact like a little child and be prepared to give up every preconceived notion, follow humbly wherever and to whatever abyss Nature leads, or you shall learn nothing!"
— T.H. Huxley

Being human has its perks. We fall in love and eat popcorn and swim in the sea. If we're lucky we get to take vacations and climb mountains, order great-tasting lattes and listen to rock stars perform in outdoor theaters. But with experiences, also come feelings. Feelings we often avoid; a habit developed at an early age.

Daydreaming in school earned us a knock upside the head, "Pay attention," the teacher said. We cried at something and mom responded, "Only babies cry." We performed skits and dad said, "Stop doing that, you look stupid." Sound familiar? For fear of ridicule or criticism, we repress our true feelings, building a shell around our unique self-expression. We end up hiding who we are.

As kids we predominantly function from the brain's right hemisphere — from the feeling, intuitive, expressive, creative sphere. Critical thinking and the analyzing process of the left brain develop later. As infants, when we wanted something, we cried or screamed or threw a tantrum. We crawled and touched things, responding to colors, sounds, shapes, textures, and temperatures. And because the linear, concept-identification, mathematical, cerebral side is not yet developed, we respond to life from the feeling perspective.

We get older and explore, only to be punished for that exploration. You put your finger in the door and it gets smashed. Ouch. That hurts. Your mother or father yells at you for getting too close to the swimming pool. Whoa. That was scary.

The right brain impulses retreat as the left brain, the processing side, takes over. This is a necessary part of cognitive and behavioral development. Without such distinctions we wouldn't survive. Without them you wouldn't be reading this now. You'd have been eaten by a saber-toothed tiger or been frozen in an ice storm or stuck your finger in the light socket.

As we proceed into the world, we're either punished or hurt ourselves for the choices we make. We create models of "right" and "wrong." As adults, we allow our creative selves to be molded by this construct of what's "good" or "right" that generally was formed by the time we are in high school. Ah, yes. High school has come back to rear it's ugly head yet again.

Ready? OK!

When I was in the 5th grade (it started early with me), I came to school one morning and dramatically announced to my class, "I'm gonna be a cheerleader. Go Kingsbury Kings!"

Cricket. Cricket.

In my small Indiana town, girls were cheerleaders. Boys played basketball. I hated basketball. I liked individual sports. Where I could express my unique self creatively. And wear cool costumes. Or dance with ribbons. I wasn't a team player. I thought it'd be fun to cheer. It was performing, after all, and I also loved gymnastics. My sister, a gymnast in high school, taught me flips, backbends, and cartwheels in our basement. (I actually think she took a perverse thrill in seeing me fall flat on my face a number of times. Maybe that was the pay-off for having to hang with her bratty kid brother.)

I took my inspiration from the Russian gymnast, Olga Korbut, in the 1976 Olympics. I sat mesmerized in front of the TV thinking, "I want to bend like a pretzel and put my feet over my head and smile while doing it (this was way before Cirque du Soleil made doing something like that seem cool). For dramatic effect, it'd even be better if I were from a mysterious Cold War country that no one really knew anything about. But I'd be happy just getting to wear those cool, red CCCP Russian National team leotards." I asked my parents why I wasn't born in a Totalitarian State. Or living behind a gigantic brick wall separating me from the rest of the world. I begged them to move to Romania so I could train to be an elite gymnast. They stared at me wondering if I'd fallen on my head one too many times. I realized I'd have to work with what I had: training behind the iron curtain of Northwest Indiana. It did sort of have its own fascist mystique. So I pretended to be a foreign exchange student from Bulgaria, greeting everyone with "Zdrasti!"

On the day of the tryouts, I just showed up. Uproar city. A special "cheerleading committee" was convened right there on the spot. Several faculty members voted on whether I'd be allowed to audition. Somehow, my request was granted. My moment had finally arrived. I marched into the gymnasium in my very short, short velour shorts and executed three flawless cheers, a number of precise jumps (the Herkie was my favorite), and a round-off, back handspring. Those skeptical faces that judged me when I first walked into the room burst into loud cheers when I finished my routine. I was pumped. It was very *Bring It On!* Team captain, Tammy Bennington and the other girls waiting to tryout looked scared. All they could do were straddle jumps and the splits. Lame.

I waited in the hallway with excitement. Look out Olga. I, too, would be talked about for years to come, influencing generations of boys who wanted to become cheerleaders.

Fifteen nail-biting minutes later, Mr. Jones, the head of the judging committee, came out from behind the closed "no students allowed past this point" doors. By the look on his face, I knew it wasn't going to be pretty. "Son," he said (any sentence that starts with "son" isn't going to end well), "you were better than any of the other girls who tried out — all 25 of them." My heart soared. I felt like I just won the Miss America Pageant having kicked ass in the talent portion with my song-and-dance rendition of Paula Abdul's "Cold-Hearted Snake." Long beat. "But," Mr. Jones continued, looking severely constipated. "We can only choose six girls. Sorry, Tony. It'd just make people feel uncomfortable to have a boy cheerlead on a girl's team."

What just happened? I was the best. Like . . . by a lot. Why couldn't I be given a chance to do what I loved?

Like Nancy Kerrigan (at the 1994 U.S. Olympic Figure Skating Trials, after being bashed in the knee by Tonya Harding's hard-lovin' boyfriend, Jeff Gillooly), I screamed,

"Why . . . ?" Mr. Jones stalked off, probably to go smoke a cigarette in the teacher's lounge and to meet up with Ms. Garrick (with whom I suspected he was having a scandalous affair). He ignored answering my question that I guess, like Nancy's, seemed rhetorical. "Why . . . ?"

And just like that — Boom! — huge realization. Certain actions in life are judged by others to be right or wrong, and we can be punished for acting out our passion, simply because people don't understand it. Other people's views could affect what I wanted to do. I thought (erroneously) there was something wrong with me. And that sucked.

I would spend the next 20 years trying to escape my *being* by doing, achieving, succeeding. As long as I excelled in something, I could compensate for my feelings of inadequacy, self-hatred and freakishness. People would only like me — and therefore I would like myself, I thought   for the things I accomplished.

Like all the other boys at my school, I ended up playing basketball instead. I hated it. And my 11-year-old self thought the cheerleaders on the sidelines sucked.

Do We Ever Really Graduate?

As we continue on our childhood developmental journey, we forge identities based on the rewards given for "right" actions and punishments exacted for "wrong." We see society reward some children for certain behavior and penalize others, and we begin to align with those actions, those paradigms (belief systems) that squash our uniqueness, encouraging us to conform. Our formative years become about assimilation. "If I do this I know I'll be rewarded. If I do that I'll be made fun of."

As the left brain is strengthened, we lose the emphasis in our right brain to create, explore, play and be spontaneous and instinctual. The more adventurous part — the seeker, the explorer — atrophies. We're told, "Boys don't cry," or "Girls shouldn't be loud or aggressive," or "Stop doing that, you're not a baby anymore." Remember these: "Fag. Sissy. Loser. Fatso. Brace-face. Trash. Whore. Slut. Retard. Zit-head. Hick. Trailer Park. Dog-face." Well, our left brain does. And it stores all of it. Only to revisit high school in our heads over and over again.

Color Me Mine

Remember when you received an "F" in elementary school for coloring outside the lines in your coloring book? Insanity. As people, as artists, we need to — we must — color wherever we want. Be a non-conformist. Color the sky green and the sea brown. Add polka dots and stripes and ignore the lines. Your own drawing is going to be better than trying to color in someone else's "correctly."

The art of living is recapturing this child-like creativity and knowing we aren't going to be punished for coloring outside the lines. All art is generated from what I believe is a transcendental place that taps into our eternal, ever youthful, ego-less selves. The word transcendental means: beyond all concepts. Love doesn't come from the left brain. Hope and compassion don't come from the left brain. Nor does passion. They're not concepts.

We love and hope, empathize, and feel passion, create and play from the right hemisphere of the brain. The left brain interferes with us expressing that natural essence of who we are.

We're moved to give money to the homeless man but don't because our left brain says we can't afford it, or that he's dirty or lazy, and we end up ignoring him. We want to tell the woman working at the neighborhood Starbucks she looks beautiful, but instead we think, "That's stupid. She'll think I'm a stalker. She's not interested in me." We shut out the possibility of miracles happening when we don't live our lives fully from a place beyond the left brain. Meaning living now.

So how do we return to this creative play without fear of being forever banished to the homeroom hell of high school?

We become aware of and cultivate the part of ourselves guiding us through life — intuition.

Homework, Week 3: Sit quietly for a few minutes and relax. Close your eyes and allow yourself to focus on your breathing. After you have quieted your mind, recall some of your earliest life experiences when you began to create a shell around your unique form of self-expression. Was there a particular event that made you want to hide who you are or was it a combination of events that slowly chipped away at your confidence? Write about it. Maybe this is the first time you've remembered a part of yourself that has been dormant. Try to remember who made fun of you or limited your capacity to create. Identify them. Write down how you feel about them. Feel the anger and sadness and pain associated with those memories. And then forgive them. Everyone's simply doing the best they can with whatever information they have available to them at any given point in life.

If certain people are still in your life (it could be a parent or brother or sister) and you've never discussed an event with them, perhaps it's time to share with them your feelings. This isn't an exercise in blaming. It's simply an honest expression of what that experience meant to you. Maybe it's too emotionally intense to talk to them in person. Perhaps you have to write a letter. Send it. Or call them. Or maybe you write the letter but choose not to send it because the actual practice of just writing your feelings down is enough. After you have shared (in whatever form works best for you), forgive them and forgive yourself.

Find the liberation in acknowledging an event in your past that may have blocked your creativity, but now that you're aware, will block you no more. In fact, at one level you should be grateful for the experience. Because without it, you wouldn't be where you are now. New insight. New you.

That's what a fully integrated artistic life is about. Finding the missing, broken, scattered pieces of the beautiful mosaic of our lives and putting them back together again to become our whole, original selves. Which is who we are when we started out on this journey, but have forgotten. It's all a circle. Never a straight line. So bless every event in your life. No matter how uncomfortable or painful. And contact the person who scares you the most. If there's still a charge — a strong reaction — in relation to this person, it means you haven't fully forgiven him or her. And if you haven't forgiven him or her, you haven't forgiven yourself.

"To me there is no greater courage than being the one who kisses first."

— Janeane Garofalo

I KNOW, BUT I DON'T WANT TO KNOW THAT I KNOW

"To really become free inside takes courage or disaster. I recommend courage."
— Christopher Reeve

Ever had a gut feeling about something? An inkling? A hunch? And then that intuition actually came to pass? You might be thinking, "Well, yeah, but I've also had a lot of other thoughts that never happened either. So it's all kind of by chance, isn't it?"

First, it's not a thought. It comes from a much deeper place within us that our mind tries to decipher and interpret through reasoning and linear thinking. Actually our mind tries to discount it. (And discount here does not mean shopping at the 99-cent store.)

Second, like most things in life, the more we seek to exercise a new muscle, the more likely we are to experience its positive effect. Use it or lose it. Isn't that how the saying goes?

The word intuition is derived from the Latin root word tutor or tutus — which means to be taught. So in-tuition is being tutored or being taught from within, internally. As an adjective — tutelary means "protecting or watching over;" a tutelary spirit is a "protective guardian." Not only are you the teacher when you intuit but you're also being protected, so to speak, by your own inner spirit.

Instinct (our inner spirit, inner teacher or guide or guardian or whatever we wish to name it) encourages heeding that voice and acting on it. If we do, we're protected, and can't go wrong because it's an expression of our unique self. When you become aware of intuition you'll realize that you are the teacher. Not me. Not Mrs. Swanson, your 10th grade English instructor. Not the guest on *The Tyra Show*. No one has your answers. Only you.

However, at the same time, every teacher — and that includes every relationship we've had — teaches us something. Every person we meet is a teacher in one way or another, and ultimately guides us to our tutor within. Whether you realize it or not, every person, every experience, every interaction brings you back to you. That's why living in this world is truly all about learning. Learning about one's Self.

Is That You Calling?

I love working with actors because I'm committed to teaching the artist to rely more and more on instinct; a place inside. Not externally; not something affected by the prejudices of others, or even our own prejudicial thoughts (which in turn have been prejudiced by others). Not by magazine articles, not by TV, not by the news or the "experts." We're being taught by something that is beyond thought. It's an internal voice telling us what to do in the moment. Instead of distrusting it, I'm getting students to act on it. In doing so, the pure potential of the moment reveals itself. By ignoring it, we miss the call to creative action.

But of course, we're conditioned to ignore our own inner voice. It's not easy to find. It can't be measured or "proven;" can't be taught by textbooks. How do you teach people to learn and understand what a voice inside them means?

Many have misidentified their "true voice" as the mind, which is really the origin of reason. (And I might argue that it's often the origin of insanity because of the destructive lies the mind tells us about ourselves.) Isn't it ironic that the true voice of reason — our inner guide — doesn't come from reason (the mind) at all? It comes from a place deep within us. We can't attribute it to a certain location. We can't point to our head and say it's coming from there. It's the voice that goes beyond reason. In fact, it will often fly in the face of reason — which is why it can be so dangerous. Dangerous — as in moving us out of our comfort zone.

We do so many things in life to ignore our inner voice. We call our best friends for advice. We make decisions based on what other people tell us is in our best interest. That's the craziest idea. How can someone else know what's best for me? How can I tell someone what's best for him? We doubt our own inner navigational system. We doubt our own wisdom and sense of inner knowing. Some of us don't even know we have one. But we all do.

If I Knew I Would Tell You

I used to say, "I don't know," (a lot!) when someone would ask me a question I wasn't ready to face. Maybe I was dating a guy and a friend would ask, "Well, what do you think about him?" I'd stall for time and backtrack and make up all sorts of excuses to avoid the truth. "I don't know," I'd whine. The truth was, I did know. I wasn't being fulfilled but I was too scared to say it. Or I was getting scared about the intimacy. Or I didn't want to face the truth that I needed to be honest with my feelings. I asked a friend recently who was miserable in her relationship, "Why don't you break up?" Her response, "I don't know."

Wrong answer. We do. Always. Sometimes the truth of what we're feeling is buried so deep underneath layers of fears and doubts and insecurities that we don't seem to have access to it.

But if we get quiet we'll hear an answer much more specific than "I don't know."

If I keep saying, "I don't know," I'm buying myself time. I really don't want to deal with my feelings. Someone might get hurt; it might get awkward. I'd rather tread water than fess up to the truth that I do know. Or I'm hoping the matter will just take care of itself. I'm hoping that in avoidance, the thing will go away. In actuality, our knowing forces us to step into the truth of that situation and confront it head on. This is what creates our own spiritual and emotional development.

Our ego doesn't want us to get clear on certain subjects; it keeps us confused and in doubt. It wants us to stay in the drama of things unexamined and safe. If we know the answer to something then we have to take steps to *move* in the direction of that knowing.

So why do we procrastinate? Because it requires letting go of the form of the false world the ego has created to keep us "in control" and safe. And that world is very, very important to us (the ego part of us). Sadly, it leaves us unfulfilled. Uninspired. Unmotivated. And even when we're miserable, our rational mind tries to convince us that our misery is better than acknowledging what we do know.

If we listen to our instinct we risk evoking a new, empowered part of ourselves to which we may have never related. Stepping into the world from that liberating place of knowing bears a certain amount of responsibility. We can't fall back on the "I don't knows" and continue to rationalize and make excuses for our predicaments. The "I don't knows" provide an out; we never have to face the things that terrify us the most, and in so doing, discover that we have the strength and the courage to overcome our most fearful challenges.

Isn't it funny that the universe seems to give us exactly what we're trying to avoid, but also what we most need to overcome to attain our new level of awareness and evolution? Ignoring and avoiding our inner truth doesn't eliminate our pain; it prolongs it.

I Don't Know = I *Do* Know, But I'll Pretend I Don't

So "I don't know" may sound pretty good when we really just don't want to deal with stuff. But stop and ask yourself, "What am I avoiding?" Maybe you want to leave your boyfriend who treats you like dirt. Or take a dance class. Or start your own business. Or confront your best friend for lying to you. Or fire your agent. Then ask yourself, "Why aren't I?" If the answer is "I don't know," listen for the *second* answer. "No one will love me. I'll be alone. I'll never find another girl. What if I fail? What if I make a mistake? I'm not ready. I'm not talented enough. I don't have anything (or anyone) else lined up yet."

So what? Our instinctual, all-knowing part wants us to take the leap. It's telling us our life depends on it. Or rather the life we *want* depends on it. It wants us to take risks, to evolve and transform. It's our higher Self urging us forward. It trusts that we're strong enough to overcome our fears. Talented enough to make something fabulous. Beautiful enough to be loved. But the ego — with its cleverly disguised "I don't knows" — sabotages us. Who are we going to listen to?

We can always justify our position or lot in life. We can always rationalize why we're stuck or unfulfilled, or defend why we're not doing more of what we want, or explain how everyone is against us. And these might all be legitimate complaints. Excuses. Reasons to be reasonable.

But do they make us happy? Do they excite us? Do they motivate us to explore the unknown areas of our life? In short, are we thriving?

I tell my students that instinct in acting, as in life, comes from a motivation beyond time. It's in the now. When they're working on a scene and have an instinct to do something and then stop themselves from doing it — like the instinct to slap their partner, let's say, and then they do nothing — they've moved from the power of the moment into the left brain's explanation of a moment. They're no longer acting now. They're talking about the moment that is now forever gone. At one point the instinct created an opportunity to go deeper but instead of surrendering to it, the actor denied it.

Missed moments. Like life. The more we think about doing what we feel, or question whether we should ("I don't know"), then we've already lost the opportunity (and the gift) that instinct has created in the moment. It's gone. Never to be repeated. Empowerment comes from seizing the moment; not doubting it, questioning it, negating it. But acting on it before it moves away from us.

Don't fret. The beautiful thing is there's always another new opportunity presenting itself. In creativity, there are always more inspired moments waiting to be birthed if we just say yes to them. Life is kind. Even though we repeatedly get in our own way, doubting our choices and second-guessing ourselves, we are always an instinct — an intuition — away from a new, extraordinary possibility. Life doesn't keep score. It keeps presenting new opportunities.

Like I said, life is circular. Thank God.

Homework, Week 4: This week, when you have an instinct, act on it. Don't wait. Become aware of the silent voice within compelling you forward.

You may wake up one morning and have the strong desire to take a cooking class. Perhaps in the past, when flashes of insight revealed themselves, you discounted them as impractical, or inconvenient, or too expensive, or ludicrous, or too scary. This time, don't wait. You're being prompted to take action. You don't need your own private invitation. In fact you're getting one: your Self is urging you to listen. As writer, Johann Wolfgang von Goethe, said, "Whatever you can do or dream you can, begin it. Boldness has genius, power and magic in it." What are you waiting for?

Since week two, you may be more familiar with the inner voice prompting you with new, creative ideas. They may be "ah-ha" moments. They may be inklings, or a voice that's urging you to "do this." Whatever it is, follow it through this week. See it through into the next phase.

This will require physical action. If you keep getting an idea for a novel and you keep ignoring it, this week sit down and start putting pen to paper. You don't have to finish it. It doesn't even have to be any good. The important thing is that you are taking the inner impulse out into the physical world and acting on it. Whatever it is — no matter how outlandish — take steps this week toward experiencing that thing in your material world.

Watch what other creative ideas and inspirations will be born because of it.

"Ultimately we know deeply that the other side of every fear is freedom."
— Marilyn Ferguson

YOUR LIFE IS OVER HERE, NOT OVER THERE

"There are cycles of success, when things come to
you and thrive, and cycles of failure, when they
wither or disintegrate and you have to let them go
in order to make room for new things to arise, or
for transformation to happen. . . . It is not true
that the up cycle is good and the down cycle bad,
except in the mind's judgment."
— Eckhart Tolle

Honoring Process

Sometimes life seems interminable. I mean, really. Life's so short — it's over in the blink of an eye — and yet on certain days when I'm stuck in my own drama, it feels like it goes on forever. It's on days like these I think of the Kate Bush song:

If I only could
I'd make a deal with God
And I'd get him to swap our places
I'd be running up that road
Be running up that hill
With no problems

Oh, yes. If only I could switch places with someone who has no problems. Is there anyone out there? Because sometimes it feels as if I've scrambled up one damn mountain only to find a much larger one in front of me. *WTF?*

Such is life. Never finished. Never complete. Just when we get to one peak, we're forced to scale a new one. We seem to arrive — at the fulfillment of some goal in life — only to realize it's not an ending, but a new beginning, at a different altitude. A new situation. A new level. And sometimes — which is really annoying — it's the *same* situation but with a different window dressing. How can I be *here* again?

It's at times like these if someone says to me, "The journey is the destination," I might smack them. After I recover from my apoplectic fit, and count to 10, I stubbornly admit that yes, indeed, life is always in process. There's no other way around it. Half the mastery of life is to understand how that game is played. And accept it.

"Transformers! Robots in Disguise . . . Transformers! Change Before Your Eyes."

Not the movie. The toy. When I was a kid, I'd buy additional parts to affix to my original Transformer (I spent a lot of my allowance on extra pieces), so it could become an airplane or a Shogun warrior or a gigantic spider or something like that. But the cool thing is, they *morphed.*

Change means "to remove or replace; to substitute one thing for another; to make different." One part has to be exchanged, dropped or substituted for something else. Having one thing excludes having the other. I have "changed." I am no longer this, I am that.

Transformation means "to grow into or evolve into new conditions, natures." People — like Transformers — don't change. They transform. It's not semantics. To become something "else" we have to first transform from something that no longer suits us. Yet once we have evolved, the pre-existing condition will still be there. It's part of who we are, of what makes us unique. Like the Transformer, I can add plastic pieces to make a flying monster truck, but remove the pieces and the original Transformer is still there.

Our pre-existing conditions are what initiate the transformation in the first place. To transform a drinking problem into sobriety, for example, we first have to identify the condition called alcoholism. That condition is creating the transformation. Once we become sober we haven't "changed." We're still an alcoholic. However, we've transformed our addiction to alcohol into health and well-being. Transformation becomes life's evolution.

Look at nature. A butterfly has a period of chrysalis while it's transforming from a caterpillar. A burnt forest over time is transformed from a barren wasteland into a field of grasses and wild flowers, and eventually gives way to a new growth of saplings, which in turn, will grow into new trees. In fact, if you look at nature's incredible resiliency in turning man-made disasters into new environs that birth and ultimately sustain new life, you can understand that the nature of transformation occurs only by utilizing present conditions. Nature metamorphosizes.

So, the parts of ourselves that we are most scared of — or hate — are the things we actually *need* as catalysts. Stop hating yourself for having them, and simply become aware of them. This is the first step.

Getting Unstuck

Most of us get stuck in life because the ego will do whatever it can to keep us from embarking on a journey into the unknown. Taking action forces us to leave the comfort and safety of what we've spent years protecting, perfecting and identifying with: our faults, problems, fears, opinions, hurts and drama.

A student, Cindy, said she was stuck. "I don't commit to anything but Häagen-Dazs ice cream," she moaned. She doesn't return phone calls or follow up with people who are interested in her for certain projects. She often leaves her scene partners scrambling and she doesn't prepare for class. Do I smell a self-saboteur?

Then Cindy had an epiphany. "I'm a commitment-phobe." Give that girl a gold star! But now what? If she sits in front of the TV and inhales the double fudge Dove Bar, or gets drunk, or reaches for the pack of cigarettes because that's what she habitually does, it's not going to matter. Transformation occurs by starting to move beyond what we habitually do. And by rejecting what we normally reach for to get us through the feelings or experiences that ordinarily shut us down.

That is hard. It takes work. We've conditioned ourselves to certain habits. They make us lazy or complacent, or, in my case, a whiner. (Would you like a glass of red wine, white wine or Tony *whine?*) We become so linked to our habit that the habit feels as real as our left ear. Before we know it, we wake up 10 years from now — if we're lucky to realize this at all — to discover our habits have forged our lives.

> "*Sow a thought, and you reap an act; sow an act, and you reap a habit; sow a habit, and you reap a character; sow a character, and you reap a destiny.*"
> — **Charles Reade**, *novelist*

Scary. *Make it all go away, Mommy!*

Actors are always asking me, "Tony, what can I do more of to make me a better actor?" They think homework, strict scene analysis, character histories, memorization of lines, costumes and wigs (!) and lots of props are going to help them expose more of themselves, and become better actors. That other stuff is like putting a band-aid on a gaping, bloody, festering open wound. *Hello! It's still bleeding. Call 9-1-1.*

"The real work occurs when you aren't 'working'."
—**Roger Ebert,** *film critic*

The real work is evoked when we examine who we really are. The parts of ourselves we don't allow to surface. The parts of ourselves that we shut down or shut out by letting an unconscious habit lull us into numbness or boredom or defeat or limited-view thinking.

Call an agent or write a monologue or pick up that guitar or take a pottery class or book a trip to Thailand or learn French or give up excuses for a day. Do the thing we are jealous of other people doing that we constantly complain we can't do and then question why we say negative things about ourselves. Question why we let our thoughts run the show. Question why we've given up on our dreams. In other words, go beyond what we know ourselves to customarily do.

Hello . . . Your Life Is Waiting

Is this you? You wake up at noon having stayed up late partying the previous night. ("That's the last time I'm going to stay out until 4 A.M.," you say to yourself.) By the time you get going, it's two o'clock. You intended to get a meeting with a talent agent. Or begin that novel. Or to work on that new song. But a friend calls and asks you to go for coffee. You kill another hour talking about all the things you "should" be doing but aren't.

You grab some lunch and watch some mindless TV. You log onto Facebook and kill another hour looking at other people's wall posts, reading about what *they're* doing when you could be doing it instead. You go the gym, which re-invigorates you and gives you a new resolve to really get some work done.

You return home. Silence. It's just you and you. No distractions. You feel anxious. Or bored. Desperate. Or sad. You spin tales in your head of worst-case scenarios. You take the "brain drain train." Next stop: Desperate City. Before you know it, you've descended into an abyss of fear and loathing. Denials and excuses. Resentment and despair.

You take a nap. When you wake up, you're too groggy to do any work and feel grumpy and unmotivated. Your dark thoughts have taken roost and you've pissed away yet another day of possibility. Since today was already a washout you decide to go out drinking with your friends and start again tomorrow.

Sound familiar? Hello, *Groundhog Day.*

But it also holds the opportunity for transformation. But before we explore how we can transform, let's take a quick look at silence and why it scares the shit out of us.

The Loudness Of Silence

Silence threatens our ego self and the self-dialogue (that would be — *the lies*) it wants us to believe. The moment we're quiet, we're forced to reckon with the feelings and thoughts we have about ourselves. But often it's too damn loud.

The first time I was planning on taking a 10-day meditation retreat near Yosemite I freaked out before I actually got there. The program consisted of getting my lazy ass up every morning at 4 A.M., 12 hours of daily meditation (done in intervals between meals, which consisted of no dinner at all), and observing absolute silence for the entire retreat. Oh yeah, and obviously no alcohol. Or communication with the outside world. Or sex. Even with yourself.

"What?" I heard myself saying. "No talking?" My family was skeptical that I'd last a day. But I was most concerned with what the silence would bring up. I remember having a panic attack the day before I left, thinking that living without language, sound, or words — having no communication for 10 days — would rip me from who I thought I was. I'd go crazy and return to my family a lunatic. I'd lose myself. I'd lose "Tony."

Once I got there, my fears were alleviated. I loved the silence. I discovered the part of me that was not my thoughts or voices inside my head. I discovered who I *am* is not what I say about myself. Or even think. It's something greater than the mind's chatter and concerns and fears.

Amuse Me! Distract Me! Entertain Me! Feed Me!

We often aren't able to access this fundamental state of who we are because the ego and all its needs is constantly clamoring for attention.

Sometimes when I arrive home from having a really bad day, instead of sitting down and taking a few moments to breathe and reflect on the day's events and how I dealt with certain situations (and how they could have been handled more compassionately;

less fearfully), I try to avoid the feelings the silence may bring by cluttering myself with excessive noise and stimulation.

I flip on the TV. I go to my computer and check emails. "How can I have no emails?" I think, "I last checked my CrackBerry 10 minutes ago. Nobody loves me. I'm not doing enough." Or I open the fridge and stare at the contents. "Damn. No chocolate? Sugar? Caffeine? No!" I tell myself, "I'm off coffee. But I really want some. Now! I need my fix. Should I run to Starbucks?"

I'll do anything to keep the stillness at bay. "I'm bored. The gym? It's too late and I'm too tired. Masturbate? I did that this morning. Read some mindless magazine? Play a video game? Watch MTV?" These are desperate times. I click on the computer and troll the internet to distract me. "A little gossip never hurt anyone," I rationalize, as I go to a number of popular sites, numbing myself.

I'm fully aware when I'm tuning in to something external to tune out the internal. And sometimes I do it anyway. I'll call my best friend and talk about nothing for two hours. That's what friend's are for, after all. To listen to our neurotic ramblings when we don't want to face ourselves.

But when I'm brave enough, I stop avoiding myself. I welcome the stillness, and feel less neurotic and stressed than if I had binged on chocolate or had a triple-espresso-shot latte. The silence offers a respite from my "monkey mind" and invites me to be gentler with myself. I get a better perspective of the things troubling me.

Is Silence Really Golden, Or Can I Just Have *Wheel Of Fortune* On In The Background?

Going into the silence can be hard. Its unknown quality seems scarier (and potentially *louder*) than the garbage we tell ourselves. Ironic, huh? To achieve a deeper level of silence within we first have to maneuver through layers of louder and uglier noise our minds throw at us. That's why we tune out. Although eventually we arrive at a deeper sense of ourselves, the journey can sometimes seem harrowing. That's why we watch reruns of *The Bachelor* instead. (I want the rose, damn it!)

The next time you feel triggered, tell yourself this, "I'm going to do something different. Not because Tony tells me I should, but because I can feel when I'm tuning out. Okay, so I'm turning off the TV. Now what? Oh crap. I'm starting to feel things. I'm not sure I like this. That Snooki sure distracted me. Watching the 'real' housewives made me feel numb. It was easier tuning into those Kardashians and their 'problems.' Now I feel bored and lonely and depressed. Breathe. It's okay that I feel these things. I'm usually not even aware that I have them. I'm going to work with what I'm thinking and feeling. Shit. I'm calling myself 'a loser' a lot. And 'stupid.' Where do these thoughts come from? Are they keeping me from being who I really want to be? Do they make me feel good? Are they the truth?"

They aren't. Transformation begins the moment we catch ourselves in the lie, and decide to do something about it.

Be kind to yourself. Some days we'll get hooked into old patterns. As we work a new muscle, it will be easier to do other things that free us from the old response system.

Call Me Crazy

People think creating art is about escaping. It's not. It's about investigating who we are, and revealing that to others. And who in their right minds would want to do that?

Think about it. What we're asked to do as artists is a little whacked. It runs counter to how we defensively survive in life. Who wants to go inside and explore the deep, frightening, hidden, ugly parts of ourselves (and the beautiful, sexy, and empowering parts) and then share them with an audience only to be judged and criticized and rejected and objectified? Well, actors do, of course. And musicians and singers and dancers and painters and poets and writers and sculptors. Anyone who creates anything with consciousness and heart.

It's a tad sadomasochistic, but for those of us who need to create, it's the only way. It's *the* way. It's part of our nature and even though we may try to avoid this introspection in our "real" lives, authentic art evokes it out of us anyway.

I once had a student who said he was going through a "hectic" and "insane" time in his life and therefore didn't want to engage emotionally in his work. *What?* You're going to have to deal with all of it. For artists, it's not about trying to get through rough patches and after we've "conquered" them, going to acting class or facing our blank canvas or music sheet with a clean plate.

First of all, life doesn't work that way. We will never have a clean plate. It's always going to be full, and sometimes messy and hot and steaming, and other times cold and lifeless. But it's still full. It's still our life.

Second, we want all this stuff going on while working. Our emotional life is all we have to draw from as artists. If we wait for the clouds to clear we miss the opportunities. Stop compartmentalizing. Stop putting things on the backburner for a "better" time. There is no better time. There's only now. Get in the game of life. Stop telling yourself that you need to have it all together first or need all the answers before you jump in. Stop saying "no" to where life is trying to take you.

Once we're in the water, we'll realize we're not going to drown. Far from it. We're going to be carried by the current.

It'll get easier. And more fun. And before we know it, the things we were avoiding suddenly don't have the same fear attached to them. Why? Because we've faced them. And in doing so, we've blessed them and let them go.

And we'll actually be grateful they came into our lives. The bad habits, the mean girlfriend, the unsupportive sibling, the lousy agent, the repetitive compulsions, the failed project, the unreturned phone calls, the broken romance. Why?

Because they were the catalysts for a tremendous transformation.

Homework, Week 5 (Part I): This week, stop reading popular entertainment magazines (and gossip websites). Ever notice they often make you feel terrible (because the websites cash in on other people's suffering)? And they also leave us strangely empty and unfulfilled? They inflame our struggle with "compare and despair." I compare myself to someone famous and to where I think I should be in my life or career, and despair because I'm not at the same place George Clooney was at my age. Or Penelope Cruz.

When we read these magazines we're already at a disadvantage. That's because everything's airbrushed, including the stories. We're comparing ourselves to illusions. Celebrities' lives are glamorized and it seems as if they don't share any of the same problems we have. Even when the cover story is about someone's recovery in rehab, doesn't it always feel as if it's "shocking" as opposed to real and painful and human and identifiable? Even their addictions seem more glamorous and exciting and attractive. Or merely something to make fun of.

The emptiness that comes from reading these treacle pieces is like the "no fat" craze a few years ago. We could've eaten 10 "zero-fat" Snackwell cookies but because they had no substance we never felt satiated. Never full. We kept gorging on them to satisfy a hunger for something more.

Do we actually remember half the stories we read in these magazines five minutes after reading them? Exactly. We tune out our own lives because everyone else's in these magazines seems better. Or maybe they're portrayed as train wrecks and for a moment we get to feel better about ourselves because we can judge other people's problems.

Instead, this week, read a poem, draw a picture, meditate, listen to a piece of music that will connect to a deeper part of you. Allow it to inspire and renew, encourage and uplift, and confirm that your path is also as important as any famous person's. People are famous nowadays for doing all sorts of things. It doesn't make them newsworthy. Or inspirational. Why are we following someone else's life because being an internet sensation seems to make their life more exciting or glamorous or profound?

I guess the real magazine litmus test is to ask yourself: "Do I feel happier, more uplifted, more inspired, more confident after reading one of these magazines?" Robert Redford puts it best when he says, "Reading about glamour is the cure when reality isn't enough."

Observe this week how we *consume* things to distract us from truly living. It could be these magazines or gossip-fueled websites or trash TV. They come in many forms. Take your pick (there are a *lot* out there). See what happens when you remove this content from your life for a week. Hopefully, you'll never waste another minute of your life again.

Homework, Week 5 (Part II): Maybe you're not the type of person who spends time reading these magazines to begin with.

So let's substitute. Find where you expend a lot of time and energy (as a distraction) by tuning out (and this will be a warm-up for another exercise we're going to do later in the book). What's your hook?

Do you watch every football game on TV? "But Tony, I love football." That's fine. But *every* game? Are you always tuned in to ESPN? Are you smoking pot? A lot? Or making lots of trips to the mall to buy things you don't need? Or watching *The Golden Girls* marathons? Are you addicted to worrying? Or gossiping? Or complaining?

For a week, see what it would be like to give these habits the kibosh.

*"When someone knocks – don't walk to the door –
Run! Because it's an experience waiting for you."*
— Pablo Castelaz

THE ENERGETIC UNIVERSE

"Life consists in what a person is thinking of all day."
— Ralph Waldo Emerson

Whenever I've faced a challenge in life and failed at meeting it, after I'm done blaming everyone but myself, I ultimately acknowledge no one's to blame *but* myself. Actually, blame isn't the right word. It's more like *taking responsibility for* the innumerable stupid things I've done. The common denominator between myself and all my life experiences is me. I acknowledge that the conditions I am experiencing are my own doing and will require my undoing to get beyond them. The outward challenges are but a projection of the inner turmoil I consciously (and unconsciously) create in my head.

Another way of saying this is manifestation (that which we experience) is the outward realization of our inner make-up. What our life looks like externally is due to what we think and believe. Most of the time we're creating unconsciously. We aren't aware that toxic thoughts — obsessing about negative experiences, holding on to resentments and anger, not being able to forgive — are attracting conditions that will support and fuel these thoughts.

Life is about becoming aware of where we hold our attention and coming to terms with our inner dialogues. Some of it just ain't pretty. Welcome to being human. But don't take my word for it. Let's talk physics.

Chemistry 101

Everything in the universe — from the human body to the planets — can be broken down into the smallest structural unit of matter — the atom. The atom is comprised of smaller subatomic particles containing positive or negative currents, better known as energy. (Some science experts might argue that the quark is smaller than the atom. But for clarity, I'm sticking with the atom because it consists of atomic particles composed of even smaller things called sub-atomic particles. The quark is one.)

Are you still with me? Wake up!

Quantum physics tells us the basic building block of everything in the universe is this energy — which is our core. All things are energy particles vibrating at such an intense speed that they come together to form a mass called you or a chair or a car. Our feelings and emotions (and thoughts, since they are connected to our feelings) are expressions of energy through our human bodies. So you can say that joy is an expression or manifestation of a type of energy. Anger would be another. Compassion. Sorrow. Rage. Love.

Albert Einstein's famous equation ($E = mc^2$) showed that mass was a reflection of the total energy of an object — energy and mass are not two different things. Given a certain amount of mass, we can calculate its energy. Alternatively, given an amount of energy, we can determine its mass. So, the mass of the universe has an energetic equivalence, and the energy of the universe has a mass equivalence that we call planets, people, galaxies, etc.

From a quantum perspective, mass *is* energy. So, the tallest skyscraper in a city is actually energy even though we see a mass of steel and concrete. A tree is energy even though we only see the physical traits of the tree: it's trunk and leaves and bark and branches. Everything is both mass and energy.

"Help Me Obi-Wan Kenobi, You're My Only Hope. . . "

David Bohm, respected as one of the best quantum physicists of all time, and a protégé of Einstein, developed (with neuroscientist, Karl Pribram) a holographic theory of the universe. Both men believed that like a hologram itself, our world and everything in it are light waves projected from a level of reality beyond space and time as we know it. Just like each piece of a hologram contains some information about the entire image, the holographic model suggests that there is a deeper level of reality that gives birth to all the appearances of our physical world. (If you revisit *Star Wars* you'll see the use of holograms all over the place.) When Princess Leia's projected image (with that Cinnabon hair roll!) pops out of R2-D2 asking for Obi-Wan's help, she appears as a hologram.

It's sort of like the shafts of light you see projected onto a movie screen to create the visual image. You buy the image as real — you get caught up in the drama of the hero or heroine — completely forgetting that the cinematic images are mere projections from a light source. The holographic theory maintains that there is a deeper order of existence that the traditional theory of objective reality doesn't account for. In other words, life is happening at deeper levels of reality than what we see. Life isn't just what you see outside your bedroom window.

"It isn't that the world of appearances is wrong; it isn't that there aren't objects out there, at one level of reality. It's that if you penetrate through and look at the universe with a holographic system, you arrive at a different view, a different reality. And that other reality can explain things that have hitherto remained inexplicable scientifically."
— **Karl Pribram**

So as not to lose the thread, let's try to pull some of these ideas together and get to the quantum center of it all: the mind.

I Am What I Am . . . Or Am I?

The Law of Thermodynamics says energy cannot be created nor destroyed. The total amount of energy and matter in the universe remains constant, merely changing from one form to another. If we think of ourselves as energetic beings sending out energy through words, thoughts, feelings, and actions, we may wonder, "Where does it all go? If it can't be destroyed nor preserved, what is happening to the energy I'm issuing into the world?"

Thoughts are things; energy waves or magnetic forces. When we have a thought, we're releasing its energy into the world. It attracts and gathers similar energy, drawing it back to us in some form or another.

Think about it. Everything in the material world was created through thought. For example, the person who first designed a computer came up with the idea — a thought — in his mind. The inventor of the water bottle first thought of the necessity of creating a receptacle for water in a convenient, disposable way. The resources, materials, supplies, information, and equipment needed to manifest the idea were second. We could say those things were attracted to the idea.

The idea — or thought — is causal. Not *casual*. (Like when the person you're dating says, "Let's not get too serious. Let's just keep it casual!")

Causal. It's creating (causing) the outward manifestation, or effect, in our material world.

Ummmm . . . Who Made That A Law? Not Me

Now this leads us to the very popular, yet much made-fun-of "law" in today's culture; The Law of Attraction.

First, the word, "law" seems so loaded doesn't it? So dramatic. So *woo woo*. This "law" is not like a state law; if I run a red light I'm going to get a ticket. Busted. It's not that type of law.

And it's also not a quantifiable, matter-based scientific law like the Laws of Gravity, or Relativity, or Newton's three Laws of Motion, or Heisenberg's Uncertainty Principle.

Maybe the easiest way to examine this point, for now, is to do away with the word "law" completely and describe it in a different way: "Thoughts are causal." Because they are.

History 101

Oh, Lordy. First chemistry, now history? Two subjects I ignored in school. I never thought history was important — life's happening now after all. But in relation to belief systems and how meaning gets lost over time, let's take a look at the historical understanding of creative thought to get a better grasp of what we're talking about when we think of causality.

The ancient teachings of *Vedanta* state that all of human nature is Divine and that our purpose is to realize our oneness. Vedanta (which comprise the oldest Sanskrit literature and the oldest Hindu philosophies) explores the understanding that our world is created through thought.

"Samsara (the world) is no more than one's thought. With effort one should therefore cleanse the thought. What one thinketh, that one becomes. This is the eternal mystery."
— The Upanishads *(verse 3.4)*

These texts were created sometime during the first millennia. Not a bad way to get the party started. (Although the actual Vedic/Upanishadic era can be traced back as far as 6,000 BCE.) That's *old*.

Around 3,000 BCE, the short and cryptic text known as *The Secret of Hermes* or *The Emerald Tablet* tried to show us the way. Why don't we ever listen?

"As above, so below. As within, so without."
— Hermes Trismegistus

Sometime between 563 BCE to 500 BCE it was perhaps said best.

"All that we are is the result of what we have thought. The mind is everything. What we think we become."
— Guatama Buddha

Maybe he was on to something. But let's fast forward to some of our modern thinkers.

> *"A human being is a part of the whole, called by us the 'Universe', a part limited in time and space. He experiences himself, his thoughts and feelings as something separated from the rest, a kind of optical delusion of his consciousness. This delusion is a kind of prison for us, restricting us to our personal desires and to affection for a few persons nearest to us. Our task must be to free ourselves from this prison by widening our circles of compassion to embrace all living creatures and the whole of nature in its beauty."*
> — Albert Einstein

Many present-day scientists believe thoughts are creative. John Wheeler, the physicist who coined the term "black hole," has maintained, through the Participatory Anthropic Principle, that the universe itself wouldn't exist if we weren't here to observe it; consciousness is needed before something can be created.

Hello Kitty

A number of scientific experiments also prove that a scientist's observation of certain experimental trials can determine and affect the outcome of such trials. Erwin Schrödinger's famous thought experiment — Schrödinger's cat — proved that if an event remains unobserved then it remains in a state where all possibilities exist, and is known as superposition. (Relax, people. The experiment was theoretical. Schrödinger killed no kitties.) By hypothetically putting Hello Kitty in a box, along with some radioactive material that if it decayed would trip a lever breaking a vial of hydrocyanic acid and therefore virtually turning our feline friend into Goodbye Kitty, Schrödinger showed that the world of matter isn't actually as unmovable and fixed as we think it is. The act of observing suggests that the nature of reality *changes* because of that observation.

In the famous double-slit experiments first done in the 1800's where light was shown to be both a wave *and* a particle, scientists demonstrated that light is a wave of energy when we don't observe it and a particle of physical substance when we do. When observing subatomic particles, a scientist's thoughts and intentions actually *change* the particles' behavior. In other words, we, as the main participant in each of our lives, can manipulate and change the outcome of our lives through thought, consciousness, and awareness.

In medical circles, the power of thought is demonstrated through placebo experiments. It has been proven time and again that people taking a placebo medicine often show the same healing results as their counterparts who actually take a real drug to combat their symptoms or illness. The mind's belief in the healing power of the drug facilitates the healing. Not just the drug.

And finally, the leading artists of today (and throughout history) illustrate through their art (if not scientifically, then artistically and philosophically) the nature of our reality and our creation of that reality. Have you seen *The Wizard of Oz? The Matrix? Inception?* Maybe you should revisit *Groundhog Day, Contact,* or *The Truman Show.*

When the biggest-grossing movie of all time discusses ideas as a vast network of energy, interconnectedness, the matrix of thought, belief systems, the oneness of our universe, and how our own disconnect from these truths suggests an "insanity that must be cured," — socially and culturally — we are experiencing a sea change.

The beauty of James Cameron's *Avatar* is that it borrows and builds on a lot of these ancient teachings I've mentioned. The

Na'vi tribe harkens back to our own Native Americans' connection to the earth and respect for nature. Their greeting, "I see you," is a play on the ancient (yet still current) Sanskrit greeting, "Namaste," which is basically recognition of one's true, higher Self as well as that in another person. "Your spirit and my spirit are one." Or "I see the Light in you as you see the Light in me."

We are more than our bodies. We are more than the thoughts we think about our bodies. The goal here is to start connecting to a deeper part within ourselves, and align our creative thoughts with a part of ourselves that is not the ego.

Synchronicity

Einstein believed that our thoughts are creative, revealing to us the future we will experience if we continue to think them. "All of this is swell," you might be thinking. "But Einstein had crazy hair and a weird fashion sense. And *Avatar* was just a movie. Where's the proof that thoughts are causal?"

Well, let's take a look at the seeming haphazardness of synchronous thoughts at play in our life. A synchronicity means two or more "seemingly random" events that are unrelated and cannot be linked through conventional causality, occur simultaneously in a "coincidental" way. So they become "synchronous" because the events are unlikely to occur together by chance.

The last time I was in India, I had a very strong random (or was it?) thought of the famous castle in Germany commissioned by the eccentric Ludwig II of Bavaria in the mid-1800s. He called the place Neuschwanstein (that's a mouthful) and it had more rooms than a Holiday Inn on Route 66 with a decorating style straight out of *Queer Eye for the Straight Guy* on crack. Can someone say glitter?

Anyway. This is an odd thought to have while traveling in a rickshaw in Mumbai (or maybe it wasn't, because our thoughts are often random). When I checked into my hotel (which itself was an actual castle!), you can imagine my shock when I noticed that the plastic water pitcher next to my bed (it looked like the kind of plastic container my mom used to make Kool-Aid in when I was a kid) had a worn sticker of Neuschwanstein Castle (!) on the front.

What are the odds of this occurring? I had to be given that *exact* room (not to be occupied by any other guests at that *exact* time) which contained that *exact* water pitcher with that *exact* picture and it had to be in an *exact* place where I would see it. It's so unique that it defies a simplistic dismissive comment such as, "That's just coincidence."

The meaning of a synchronicity is up to you to explore and uncover. That's part of your life's unfolding. What does something like that mean to you in your life right now? From a universal perspective, this example demonstrated to me that although the cosmos appears enormous, in truth, everything begins and ends in one place: the mind. Or rather, consciousness. From an individual, personal perspective, it connected me to my memory of a childhood trip my family took to Neuschwanstein. There I was, many years later, staying at a castle about as far away from Germany as you can get, and yet both places were connected through my memory and a visual clue stamped on a plastic jug.

If you begin to open your eyes, you will see the universe is trying to speak with you all the time. And I have found that it has an unbelievably benevolent sense of humor.

As wonderful as the synchronicity I experienced in India was, maybe the entire meaning of that event hasn't played out yet. Maybe there are more pieces to the puzzle still taking shape. If we stay open to the idea that something miraculous might be at work governing our existence, other signs and symbols will appear on our path. We just have to stop demanding that we get all the answers right now.

I Was *Just* Thinking Of You!

When we think of someone out of the blue — with no attachment — and suddenly that person shows up in our life, it can be a shock to the system. Surprising. Wonderful. We say, "Oh my gosh! I was just thinking about you and here you are!" This has happened to all of us. Some more than others. At these times, doesn't it feel as if thought actually *is* causal?

The argument often presented is that it's just a "coincidence." But if the definition of coincidence is that of an accidental, or an uncanny or unexpected event happening in tandem with another event, then is it really an "accident" or coincidence if it *keeps* happening? The interesting aspect is that as soon as we begin to notice that we're having synchronicities, we'll begin to experience more of them.

This is also an example of the energetic component of thoughts. The more attention we give to something, the more we see evidence of that thing showing up in our experience.

Think of the possibilities. What if our thinking is part of a causal chain of events in which we play an active role? What if it is part of a larger collective, a universal matrix of thought? That each individual mind is actually part of *one* (mind)? A storehouse of interconnected information and infinite intelligence that all of us can access. Since all thought is creative, it's about our tapping into unseen creative potential. Amazing stuff.

But how do we get there?

We have to stop doing things that prevent us from being connected to it. Things like doubting or dismissing the mystery of possibility. We have to let go of fear and negation; qualities that make us react and operate on autopilot. We have to stop buying into conditioned beliefs that cut us off from wonder and the unknown, preventing us from exploring new ways to open our minds to new ideas and paradigms. Sadly, the repetitive thoughts our trained, conditioned minds generate on a daily basis provide us with little more than what we've been telling ourselves for years. They are *closed systems*.

Where's My Shiny New Car, My Mansion On The Beach, And My Soul Mate?

Part of our challenge in life is that as we identify ourselves primarily through the ego, we don't have access to anything else as reference points to who we are. As I mentioned earlier, a new awareness has occurred in our culture recently. Sadly, it's still being deciphered through the prism of the ego and therefore, once again, misunderstood.

For example, because of the huge success of the phenomenon, *The Secret*, the principles surrounding the Law of Attraction became convoluted. Critics scoffed at the simplicity of the book's premise that we have the power to manifest whatever we think about and desire in life. But it's equally simplistic to think that thoughts *aren't* causal. The irony — which critics seem to have overlooked — is that *everything* we see in the material world that's been created by man (from an iPad to an igloo) was *first* created as a thought. So where does that leave us?

Fans of the book only made things worse by fixating on material things desired by the ego, implying that someone could merely think of something and it would magically appear. "I want my brand new BMW! I'm thinking about it. Where the @%$@# is it?"

Skeptics pounced again on this implausibility, taking a glib overview. If someone had the power to create his or her own reality, why would they choose to live in squalor, or suffer from incurable disease, or constantly be abused, or go hungry and homeless?

Such a cynical response is an oversimplification of a physiological, psychological, emotional and spiritual matrix that involves many components of our own thought-making machine: our mind. People don't want to examine their mind. They want to blame others for their problems. They don't want to look within themselves.

Say It Isn't So

If we were honest about the myriad thoughts we had on a daily basis (from our wildest fantasies to our most debased perversions, from our highest aspirations to our most destructive obsessions), each of us would be clinically diagnosed as psychopathic.

Who me?

I mean, seriously. If you really listen to all the things your mind tells you, you'd have to admit that *you're nuts!*

Thankfully, just like having a desire for a new BMW we don't actually think we'll ever get (and so we won't), most of our errant thoughts carry very little emotional leverage and therefore aren't experienced in the way we often dream them. And maybe this is a good thing. And for many of us, our lives seem almost haphazard and directionless – partly because of the chaotic thoughts we continue to think.

But our thought-making mind doesn't begin and end with just our own internal make-up, our own individual consciousness. There are a number of other consciousness-shaping influences that determine our own state of mind.

There's cultural consciousness. Why does an indigenous Amazonian group of people living in the Envira region of Brazil (who have been discovered to be one of Earth's last un-contacted native tribes) — have zero understanding of what an airplane is? When a plane flew over their previously hidden dwelling deep in the rainforest last year, the tribe raised spears and bows and arrows in a defiant gesture to ward off this strange, unfamiliar creature. They have no cultural reference to what a plane is. It's not a part of their collective cultural consciousness. And yet you and I can't even imagine *not knowing* what a plane is.

There's societal consciousness. Certain mores and traditions that have been part of a society's history and culture create the thought-systems of who we are within that society. Rituals and beliefs, traditions and pastimes are passed on from generation to generation, forging biases and predilections within our consciousness. Generally, societal consciousness is influenced by mainstream viewpoints. For example, a person may not empathize with marginalized groups within a culture and not support their equal rights. This person is someone whose acquired social consciousness has been shaped by the prejudices and fears of a society who believe in separatism. Or, if the predominant thought of a group of people is love, then those loving thoughts and the energy equivalent are shared and felt by other people in other areas. If collectively, a group of people's overriding thoughts are those of hate or war, then, those dominant thoughts will energetically affect another group's feelings, possibly engendering more feeling of hate and war within that group.

There's collective consciousness. The consciousness of every person on the entire planet; the interconnectedness shared by the human experience. We all feel pain, hope, fear, love, excitement, compassion, hate, desire. We are all connected through that matrix of human existence. Collective consciousness can be thought of as a larger extension of societal consciousness, which in turn is an expansion of cultural consciousness. It transcends regions, race, and religion, gender and age, and taps into shared human experiences. Atomically and biologically.

If you doubt it, just read what physicists say about our connectedness through history, time, energy, and atoms.

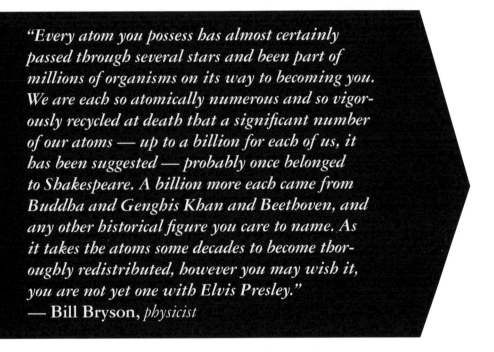

"Every atom you possess has almost certainly passed through several stars and been part of millions of organisms on its way to becoming you. We are each so atomically numerous and so vigorously recycled at death that a significant number of our atoms — up to a billion for each of us, it has been suggested — probably once belonged to Shakespeare. A billion more each came from Buddha and Genghis Khan and Beethoven, and any other historical figure you care to name. As it takes the atoms some decades to become thoroughly redistributed, however you may wish it, you are not yet one with Elvis Presley."
— **Bill Bryson,** *physicist*

And finally, there's also **universal consciousness**. The entire solar system is alive and throbbing with energy. The planet is a living, breathing organism. Everything that exists within it has some sort of transforming energy or underlying intelligence: from the paramecium to the polar bear.

> *"If the Big Bang had been one-part-in-a-million more powerful, it would have rushed out too fast for the galaxies and life to develop. If the strong nuclear force were decreased two percent, atomic nuclei wouldn't hold together, and plain-vanilla hydrogen would be the only kind of atom in the universe. If gravitational force were decreased by a hair, stars (including the Sun) would not ignite. These are just three of just more than two hundred physical parameters within the solar system and universe so exact that it strains credulity to propose that they are random. These fundamental constants of the universe all seem to be carefully chosen, often with great precision, to allow for the existence of life and consciousness."*
> — Robert Lanza, *physicist*

This brings us back to square one. Rather than negating the theory that thoughts are causal, perhaps we would be better served if we suspended our judgment and considered the *possibility* that thoughts actually are at the root of our creative universe. That we have a hand in our life's design. That what we think *does* matter.

Are You Feeling What I'm Feeling?

One way to help get there is to become aware of what we are feeling; more specifically, the thoughts that generate powerful feeling. Scientists say we can have up to 70,000 thoughts a day and 80% of them are negative. But many are also known as "soft thoughts." In other words, they don't create a strong emotional charge. We don't give much credence to thoughts such as, "I love peanut butter," or "I have to go to the gym." Unless we hate going to the gym, and then that thought probably has a distinct negative charge attached to the idea and we go have a margarita instead. (Which has the same amount of calories as a glazed doughnut, by the way. Ouch.)

When I'm discussing causal thoughts, I'm talking about those that create emotional polarity within us — either positive or negative — around a certain subject. We think of our ex and we feel rage. Or we have negative thoughts about our weight and feel hopeless. We think a friend betrayed us and feel revengeful. Or in our acting we might feel dread and inadequacy. The thoughts commingle with powerful feelings.

When we become aware of what we're feeling we become conscious of what we're putting out into the universe. And when we're aware of that, we can stop blaming our teacher, parents, ex-lover, agent, business, employees, siblings, "Hollywood," our past, and win back our power to create with consciousness.

The choice is ours. And we always have a choice.

Trick Me Once, Shame On You; Trick Me Twice, Shame On Me

The universe doesn't make judgments about what we're asking for or what it is giving us. It's not a moral arbitrator. It's not saying, "You're good. You're bad. You deserve this. You deserve that." It gives us what we ask for. That is, what we're thinking about, what's making us feel, and what we're offering — or telegraphing — to the world through emotion or feeling. Why?

Because where we choose to focus our feeling (even if it's things *un*-wanted), we create more of. The universe doesn't differentiate between reality and imagination. Whichever we choose to act from is what we increase. It's like when we tell our subconscious, "I'm going to get sick," and sure enough, in two days, we do. We're manifesting our own self-fulfilled prophecy. So goes the saying: we don't get what we wish for in life. We get what we *believe*. So whenever we have a strong desire and a contrary belief surrounding that strong desire, whichever has the strongest emotional charge within is going to prevail.

Let's say our desire is to be on a popular TV show, but our thoughts are: "I suck. I'm untalented. I'm not attractive enough. I don't have enough credits. I'm too old. I always blow my auditions." These thoughts create negative feeling within. If those feelings are stronger than our initial desire to be on such a show, then the most prevalent feeling is what's going to be manifested.

Dominant energy is *causal*. This is how we keep "sabotaging" ourselves from what we want.

Disco Days

Generally, when we have a desire we initially feel good about ("I can do this!"), we often simultaneously feel terrible because the desire also triggers a negative belief ("No you can't stupid!"). Why? Because our pre-conditioned thoughts have been formulated since we were children, having created a neural pathway in our brain. (Patterns of thought continuously repeated become habit, which creates neuroplasticity; also referred to as a "groove," which is simply interconnected neurons carrying the repeated patterns of behavior of a habit.) So when we desire something, our brain's neural groove immediately gets triggered out of habit to correspond to that desire.

The real work is to create a new brain network to replace the old, outdated, untruthful grooves, thereby reconciling our belief system with our desires. If one thought is, "I want to find my soul mate," and the other is, "I'm such a loser," which thought prevails? We don't realize that we simply foil our desires from manifesting because the negative thoughts get played like a record over and over again.

When I was a kid, I'd roller skate to a 45" single record of Rick Dees' "*Disco Duck.*" (Oh no you didn't! Sadly, I did.) I played that song over and over so many times it had scratches and worn grooves and would always get stuck right at my favorite part of the chorus: "Disco . . . Disco Duck. Try your luck. Don't be a cluck! Disco . . . Disco." I'd be twirling and spinning like a roller derby star, when suddenly that damn duck would *Scratch!* I'd have to stop my routine (Annoying!) and start the record all over again from the beginning. (Irritating!) And this only added to the record's groove deepening. (Maddening!)

Our brains are like these worn-out records. But with a much less catchy disco beat.

Re-Booting Our Brain, Re-Tuning Our GPS

It's great to have desires. We'll always have them. Even the wish of not having desires *is* a desire. We fulfill one and then desire something else. It never ends. The key to experiencing them manifesting in our life is that when we have these intense, wonderful, passionate desires to create or fall in love or be in service, try to remain in the original feeling that gave birth to the desire in the first place. Just like a car's GPS system tells us where we are heading, our own emotional bodies have an inner guidance system. Our GPS is based on feeling.

When we are feeling excited and passionate and hopeful, we are moving closer to our destination. When we are feeling irritable and angry and depressed, we are moving away from what we want. It's not rocket science here. To feel good feels good. We need to move our internal GPS system into alignment with what we're feeling. And when we feel things that throw us off course, we realign. That's the real work, because our belief system will win out over our desires every time, as its simply been in place a lot longer.

Like everything, it's a process. The work is simple: as we desire something and send the thought or feeling into the universe, and it triggers a negative belief and makes us feel badly, we stop and reconsider. Instead of the needle getting stuck in that neural groove, we change that thought and the feeling will change (and actually start building a more empowering neural pathway). Another way you can think of it is in terms of resistance (what we don't want) and flow (what we do).

"I can't find someone who likes me," is a resistant thought. It holds us in opposition to what we want — a partner. What we want is always in the flow. So how do we have the awareness to shift?

First, look at the situation from a broader perspective. From a new horizon. Sort of how your friends might view your situation from the outside looking in. "I've been single for a while but have learned a lot about myself. My ex-girlfriends have shown me things I needed to learn. I'm grateful for those experiences. I feel as if I have a lot to give. I'm funny. I'm kind. I'm sensitive. I'm a good dancer. I have style. I'm sexy. I'm macho. I'm good in bed." I bet you're smiling right now and you see, this is how you begin to realign with your desire without holding resistance.

These statements about having a girlfriend are examples of truth. They are not closed systems of thought that shut out potential. They are not lies we keep rebooting that prevent us from seeing (and feeling) the possibility from another perspective.

Finding a better way of feeling about where we are *is* truth.

Finding Your Inner Nemo

Think of the universe as generating this amazing jet stream we're all riding. Like in the movie, *Finding Nemo,* the turtles ride the ocean's jet stream and excitedly call out, "Cowabunga dude. Let's ride the wave!" But Nemo's dad fights the stream.

Each of us is born into this world to go with the flow. It's a dance. When we do, we become the spontaneous fulfillment of all our desires. If we resist riding that stream because of control, because of our conditioned way of thinking, because of fear, and we try to go upstream, we work against the current. We end up activating the negative charge within us. We create resistance. Remember the lullaby: "Row, row, row your boat, gently down the stream . . . ?" It wasn't upstream. It wasn't against the stream. Why then, as adults, do we go against this natural flowing current?

Because we don't believe it's supposed to be easy. We believe life is supposed to be about struggle and fighting against things. We battle ourselves, believing we aren't deserving of the things we desire. But the comforting truth is that even when we're fighting against our own natural flow, against life's rhythm itself, the current still carries us downstream.

But we just don't want to trust that, do we?

> *"Life is always in the right."*
> — Rainer Maria Rilke, *poet*

Finding Nemo is not called *Searching for Nemo*. It's not called *Looking for Nemo*. It's called *Finding Nemo*. Which means it's inevitable that we will arrive at the fulfillment of our desires, if we *allow* ourselves to experience them. We're all heading to the same place. We're being carried downstream. Even in our darkest days when we don't feel good about ourselves, things seem awful, and there doesn't appear to be a way out of this hole that we've dug, we're still being carried by this stream. At moments like these we need to reassure ourselves. It's safe to give up control. I can let go of the oars. Let me breathe, relax, trust.

If we ever doubt this, look at life. Even when we're trying to buck the current, take a moment to see how amazing life is. Look at all that *is* working in our lives. We're alive, and healthy. We're reading this book. We can afford a movie ticket. We can go out on dates. We can travel. Eat at our favorite restaurants. Surf the net and google something we need, receiving the answer in five seconds flat. We can go hiking or dancing or swimming. We're creating. We're pursuing our dreams.

There's a lot that is working in our lives. Our habituated tendency is to focus on all the stuff that isn't.

Why? Because we misinterpret our life's events. We create fiction out of things that we've experienced.

But we are *not* the events that happened to us.

What? I'm Re-enacting My 7th Grade Neural Groove?

As I mentioned earlier, science has shown that our habitual thoughts create neural grooves in the brain that get worn and deepened as the thoughts are repeated. They're the contaminated thoughts we've unconsciously been telling ourselves for years that get stimulated when we're in a new situation that's stressful or emotional, and create a negative emotional charge.

We have an altercation with a lover and suddenly we tell ourselves, "I'm a jerk. An ass. I constantly mess things up." Those thoughts are the lies that someone said to us when we were in the 7th grade. Our emotional exchange with our lover triggers our 7th grade neural pathway, and we're living out that experience with the schoolyard bully from 20 years ago.

Here's an example. In the 7th grade, I'd hide from Bobby Burndorf, the resident bully. (When I think about it now he was a 90-lb. weakling — I could have broken him like a pretzel — what the hell was I so scared of?) But words have power. And I believed them. And the way he bullied me, made him appear much larger than the tiny twig of a boy he actually was.

Every day after 3rd period I'd avoid going to my locker; I didn't want to pass him in the hall because if he saw me he'd tease me in front of everyone. No matter what route I'd take or how late I'd be to my next class, he always seemed to be lurking right outside the door I needed to get to. He'd see me; shout, "Fag!" and the entire hallway of students would laugh. I was paralyzed with terror. I'd literally find new paths to get to my locker to avoid him, even if it meant I'd be late to class and be called out by my teacher. Lord knows I didn't want to be known as a "fag" *and* a "snitch," so I just took it, never telling anyone why I was late.

This kid (who was scared and felt inferior *himself*) projected his fears onto me. I took them as my truth: I was "a fag." I didn't even know what the hell that word meant, but I knew it had to be bad because of the shame and self-hate I felt when everyone else laughed. I associated that word with how bad of a person I had to be for people to call me that. *Scratch!* A neural groove was born.

Societal Sponge

Present-day upsets can trigger our own past associations in the same way if we're not aware and we let ourselves react from the past.

How many times have we heard these "truths:" "Life's a challenge." "Life's hard." "You can't trust anyone." "You have to be careful." "Look out for yourself." Or they can be more personal: "Fat women are ugly." "Gays should burn in hell." "Artists are crazy." When society tries to marginalize any segment and we are part of that segment, we assume those prejudices as our truth.

Taking on these incorrect individual and societal interpretations (without even realizing we have done so) places us against the natural flow of the universe. It's not who we are.

So who we are — who we're all born as — is pure, positive, abundant, loving energy. Look at babies. Pure bliss. We're born into this world knowing at some level that this is who we are — powerful creators — and when we tap into this part, we transform consciousness. We heal.

Stop allowing the events that happened to us in 1978 to become our now. All it takes is a little bit of awareness. That's the first step.

Whatever happened to Bobby Burndorf? There's a happy ending, as there are to most stories, I think. At some point later in the year, I realized my size in relation to his and I had a light bulb moment. *Ding.* I can Kick. His. Ass. (Not condoning violence here, but sometimes you just have to stick up for yourself and not let someone treat you like dirt.)

And having muscle as a teenager is highly under-rated. One afternoon, wearing my favorite powder blue Izod sweater, pleated khakis and my un-scuffed penny-loafers (Hello. It was the '80's. Preppy was in!), I slammed his bully self up against a locker, whispering through clenched teeth with great urgency (I think I was as scared of me as he was), "If you ever call me that again, you're gonna regret it." *Snap.* He went scurrying off to class, looking over his shoulder as if the "fag" had somehow channeled Hulk Hogan with style points. *Bam!*

That's how I like to remember it anyway. Or maybe my sister pushed him up against the locker for me. Whatever the case, Mr. Bobby Burndorf never bothered me again.

Homework, Week 6: Einstein said, "Imagination is the preview of life's coming attractions." Although he dwelled in the world of quarks and neutrinos, relativity and radioactive decay, his assertion that thoughts (and the feelings associated with them) create our reality is as scientific as it is spiritual. Just read the ancient Buddhist and Vedic texts that preceded Einstein by two thousand years to see the stunning similarities. But don't take my word for it. Find out for yourselves. Transform a belief into actual *experience.* That's the way to know for sure.

The homework for this week includes a five-minute exercise to add to the five-minute meditation you are (hopefully) doing every morning and every night. After your meditation, put on some of your favorite, inspiring music. Close your eyes and take a visual journey with the music as if you were watching the cinematic story of your life. What would you like to see yourself be the star of? Flood your imagination with the most exciting possibilities you could live. (Remember, if you can imagine it, you can live it). So don't be tentative in your visualization.

If you imagine yourself living part-time in New York and Paris — don't let the left brain chime in, discounting that possibility by saying, "Ummmm... How are you ever going to be able to afford that?" You don't have to worry about the details. The details are always taken care of. So just dream it. And feel it. *Feel* what it feels like to get married on the beach to your soul mate. *Feel* what it feels like to win an award for your art. *Feel* what it's like to take a vacation to a far-away place you've always wanted to visit. Be extraordinary in your mind picturing. Don't hold back. And most importantly, always keep connecting the picture to a feeling.

At first when you start this exercise you may feel uncomfortable or scared. As you dream big, you may trigger doubts and anxiety about that happening. If that occurs, at first, work with smaller dreams. If you can't imagine your artwork being shown at a major gallery showing in New York without you getting nervous, start smaller.

Let it be a small reception somewhere in a friend's home, with a small group of people admiring your paintings and buying them. That feels good. Then you can begin moving toward bigger dreams. As you do, you'll start to wonder why you haven't been dreaming that big to begin with. Don't beat yourself up about it. Be excited that you are now at a new level in your awareness that you can ask for, and are truly deserving of more.

Do a five-minute visualization every day for the next week.

"Thought is the sculptor who can create the person you want to be."
— Henry David Thoreau

WE'VE GOT SPIRIT, YES WE DO! WE'VE GOT SPIRIT, HOW 'BOUT YOU?

> *"In everyone's life, at some time, our inner fire goes out. It is then burst into flame by an encounter with another human being. We should all be thankful for those people who rekindle the inner spirit."*
> — Albert Schweitzer

Inspiration. It's actually more than a word — it's a state of being. Inspiration means to be *in-spirit*. Which in turn means to give life or courage to, to breathe life *into* something. It means living and creating in a space that is ego-less. To be fully, vitally, optimally expressed, the way we are intended to live. Not critically or editorially. Not saying, "I suck. My work is awful." Let someone else do that. Lord knows there are enough people out there to judge us. So why do it to ourselves before we've even created it?

We, as artists, have the power to inspire others. This is what artists do. And people say art isn't relevant or important? (Sarah Palin thinks the National Endowment for the Arts is "frivolous.") What planet are they living on? When someone touches our life in a profound way, the event is an inspirational force. It means someone has evoked inspiration within us, revealing to us our ability to call upon our own courage, vitality; the spirited part of who we are.

They help open us to new experiences, encouraging us to take the next step. It's not that they consciously tap us on the shoulder and reveal these things to us — although in some cases they do.

It's more as if their inspiration lights the flickering flame within us that's not yet been ignited. But it has always been there.

We don't realize that even the smallest acts, the simplest gestures — smiling at a stranger, looking someone in the eye and saying "hello," assisting someone in a time of need, or holding the door open for someone — are inspired acts. They create a space for two or more people to engage in a shared experience. Therefore, the nature of inspiration unfolds through relationship.

Can You Relate?

Everything in this existence is defined through relationship. With ourselves, with our lover, parents, the grocer, the car mechanic. And with things: food, caffeine, money, clothing, the rainforest, the ocean. In fact, there is no "thing" in life — it's all relationship. Or rather, all the "things" in our lives are things to which we are relating.

Think of it this way. We're living in a transitory, impermanent world. Because of its impermanence there really isn't anything called a relationship, as a relationship makes something a *thing*, an entity, and makes it fixed and immovable. It becomes objectified. Nothing (*no thing*) in life is fixed. Existence itself is in a state of flux, always energetically transforming, even if these changes aren't visible to the naked eye.

The accurate way to see ourselves isn't in relationship with someone, but "in relating." Relationship is a noun, a thing. "Relating" is a verb, a process. Relationship is the past. "Relating" is now.

Jane Fonda says she changed from "a noun to a verb," when she became involved in helping other people, relating to them beyond being famous. "A verb is active and less ego-oriented. Being a verb means being defined by action, not by title."

"Everything the Buddha was teaching was replacing nouns with verbs."
— Osho, *spiritual teacher*

So we are constantly in states of becoming.

But That's Not The Way It Looked On TV!

Why do so many marriages end in divorce? Because people believe it's the finish line. We think marriage looks a certain way. The way it looks on TV and romanticized in the movies. "Wow. We're married. We made it. The finish line." But the process from engagement to marriage isn't a means to the end. It's the beginning of a new way of relating to another under the rules of matrimony. It's not a fixed thing.

One of the major causes of suffering is our steadfast adherence to an image of what we think something is supposed to look like. As long as I see someone as the coach or teacher or parent, they fulfill a label of what my belief system says those roles should be. But in my *relating* to someone who fulfills one of these parts, I allow the experience to be fluid, changing. We have a hard time with this. We reduce people to living concepts.

For example, many of us identify people who are in their 50's or 60's as parental or grand-parental; we don't think of them as sexual. We don't want to imagine them still getting it on, enjoying sex. We don't want to go there. We want to think of Nana as the sweet lady who still makes the best chocolate chip cookies in the world. The possibility that our grandmother may still be a sex goddess in or out of the bedroom is just too much. But look at Madonna who's in her 50's or Raquel Welch who's in her 70's. Or Sharon Stone, Helen Mirren, Iman, Angela Bassett, Michelle Pfeiffer, Michelle Obama, Oprah Winfrey.

People over 50 have real, sizzling sexual lives just like the rest of humanity. Some of them may rock; some of them not. Some of them are hot like Tina Turner and Susan Sarandon; Bruce Willis and Richard Gere. Some of them not so much. Just like people of every age.

The point is, sexy is not defined or limited by how old we are. Neither is French kissing, or swinging from the chandeliers, or having hot sex all night long. So why would we want to put limits on it? Similarly, we often relate to people of other cultures and ethnicities as "charming," or "unique," or "funny" because stigmatizing them a certain way allows us to ignore our prejudices and keeps them separate.

Ever notice that in many TV shows and films, supporting roles filled by minorities (such as gays, African Americans, Latinos, or Asians) are stereotypes? They become the "comic" or "non-sexual best friend." To portray a character from Pakistan in a *real* way with real desires is too provocative. We'd have to explore our own hidden fears and bigotry. Too scary to consider. Academy Award winner, Rita Moreno, recently said, "Can I tell you how many offers I've gotten to be somebody's mother or grandmother who pours the (Puerto Rican) coffee? . . . I'm not going to do that. Not at 79." So the gay guy is the "flaming non-sexual hairdresser," the Latina is the "Mexican maid," and the Native American is the "all-knowing tribal chief." Identifiable roles to make us — the masses — feel comfortable. "Oh, aren't they funny? Isn't she cute?" Well, actually no. They're just like you and me. Complex, messy, beautiful, passionate. No one is a living concept.

The Man (Or Woman) In The Mirror

We're made up of all the relating we do in life, from the most fleeting talk with a phone solicitor who harasses us for 30 seconds to the old high school nemesis making fun of us to the current lover to whom we relate intimately and with whom we credit changing our lives. Everyone has the potential to "change our life."

Every person is a mirror of ourselves. When we see someone we're attracted to, we see ourselves reflected in that person or we see certain qualities we want to develop in ourselves. This is especially true when we meet inspirational people. They seem to possess qualities that we mistakenly believe we don't have or they awaken us to our own latent qualities that we wish to develop.

Similarly, when we feel repelled by someone it's also because we see our own image reflected in that person. But who in the hell wants to admit that? It's so easy to understand why we're attracted to someone who exudes positive qualities, but we don't want to admit that the person in our writing class whom we think is "an egomaniac" is anything like us.

I know you're probably thinking, "But I'm not like him." But to deny that we, too, possess an inner miser, an inner egomaniac, an inner ass, tyrant, gossip, cheat, deviant, bitch is contrary to the universality of being human. We don't want to acknowledge these qualities because we judge them as bad or wrong. Or acknowledging them within ourselves is just too scary, so we project them onto others instead. But once again, the paradoxical nature of duality means that no phenomenon can exist without the experience of its opposite state. One characteristic may be dominating, but neither exists devoid of its opposite.

For example, let's say I've forgiven my sister for something she said that hurt my feelings. My condition of forgiveness is only possible because at some point — either to her or to someone else — I've been *un*forgiving. And as hard as it is (to the ego) to admit, if I'm honest, *every* time I've judged someone, I've either demonstrated that same quality in my own life and didn't want to admit it *or* I refuse to look at that part that resides within me that I accuse only other people of having. So when I'm forgiving my sister, I'm actually forgiving myself. That's because it's certain the very thing I'm forgiving her for, I myself have thought, felt or done a hundred times.

So demonizing someone else certainly makes it easier, doesn't it? But when you catch your own mind games, you can dismantle them. They no longer have any place to hide. We stop projecting them onto others and spend less time talking about other people's deficiencies, because we've recognized our judgments of others are really judgments against ourselves.

As artists, it's especially important to be truthful in recognizing the potentials we possess, both divine and profane. Every one of us contains all tendencies of all characters. If we didn't, we wouldn't be able to play them.

OMG! I Am Nothing Like That . . . Am I?

One of my students remarked that she could see how Tony Soprano on *The Sopranos* could murder someone, but how did James Gandolfini playing the role get to that place emotionally? I'm not sure of his personal process, but one thing I'm sure of is that Mr. Gandolfini can't deny his own human impulse to lash out or perpetrate violence. He had to acknowledge his *own* Tony Soprano within to truthfully express those aspects in his work.

If I were playing a murderer, how do I non-judgmentally explore that part of myself, even if I don't spend my days physically harming other humans? The first step is to simply acknowledge that somewhere within me dwells the *potential* to harm others. If I'm really being honest I can see that I have an inner Mussolini lurking behind this sweet exterior. It takes guts to admit that.

You mean sweet little me could unleash such rage and hate I could physically hurt someone? Ummm . . . yes. The next question would be, "Well, how do I access that?"

I despise mosquitoes. (Does anyone like them?) Growing up in Indiana during our long, hot and humid summers, mosquitoes would invariably get into my bedroom and buzz incessantly in my ears. You know the sound. It's right up there with nails on the chalkboard. I'd wake up like a cannon blast, flailing my arms in the black, moonless night hoping to strike my unseen but annoyingly loud enemies. With no luck, I'd fall back asleep (sweltering under the pulled-up covers trying to protect my exposed skin) only to be awakened a few moments later by that incessant buzz. Jumping out of bed in a rage, I'd flip on the lights and search my room like a maniac, examining the walls until I'd find the culprits. Then — *Wham!* — contact. Removing my bloody hand from the wall and seeing my smashed quarry would create such glee I'd dance around the room. This is true. (And sadly, something I'm not proud of, as I still do this as an adult.)

The point is; I've taken a spiritual vow to not willfully harm any defenseless creature. Yet when a mosquito enters my room, forget about my lofty spiritual aspirations. *Hypocrite.* Everything gives way to the primal, animal instinct in me to kill. Die suckers. It isn't pretty.

A mosquito obviously isn't human, but it's still a living creature. My intent is an example of a harmful tendency. This same inclination to willfully harm (a person or animal) begins with just the thought. It doesn't matter that a mosquito incited the rage or not. The fact is, I am certainly capable of tapping into those vengeful feelings if I were asked to play someone like Tony Soprano, who does it for a living.

"I think acting is definitely subversive. There's an anarchic quality to acting that people envy and lash out at. Actors represent a danger to society. It's that discovery of a thing in each of us that we'd rather not examine, we'd rather not touch on. And the better the actor, the closer they are to that truth, and that makes them dangerous, because it wakes ourselves up to who and what we are. Take Medea, *for example. To do a really satisfying* Medea, *truly, you have to find that part of you that would kill your own children. If you have a child who has colic, who screams for six months (because that's how long colic lasts), you will think about killing that child if you allow yourself to. Now what actress is willing to examine that? A great actress. But once she does, she communicates that to the house. She discovers what that awakens, on stage, in front of you, live, there. When she does, you do. And that is scary."*
— F. Murray Abraham, *actor*

Recently, a student in one of my classes was exploring a role in which the character has an affair with her sister's husband. It was clear the actress was phoning it in. "Tony, I hate the scene." I asked her why. She didn't give a clear answer. I finally asked, "Susan, have you ever had an affair before?" Suddenly, she burst into tears. She admitted she'd actually cheated with her own sister's boyfriend at one point in her life. Talk about too close to home.

It was a moving confession to something she wasn't proud of, and yet it happened many years ago. It was something she needed to forgive herself for doing. Her reluctance to do the scene was obvious. Because the very thing that the character faces requires the actress playing her to tap into and use her own experiences. Since she actually had this experience, it was even more immediate. When the actor's willing to work with his or her own emotional life that connects to a role, the role comes alive in a way that I think every actor desires to experience.

"It comes down to the willingness to push yourself into emotional territory that may scare you as much as it scares your audience. It's the most mysterious and the finest quality an actor can have. Let's call it fearlessness."
— **Margo Jefferson,** *film critic*

The way the actor taps into these parts and truthfully examines them is the way we all want to honestly acknowledge ourselves in our lives. When we identify those qualities within as those that we project onto others, we take a big step toward a new level of understanding that's transformative: *compassion.*

Compassion Is Projection Turned Inward

That's such a great saying. And something we need to do more of. Turn inward. A student, Erica, once remarked that a scene she was working on made her angry. It brought up issues of intimacy and sexuality she felt uncomfortable exploring. She refused to continue working on the scene. My response to her was simple: You should never be defeated by material. Ever.

The question each of us needs to ask is, "Why do I have so much resistance? Why do I dislike it so much?" In Erica's case, it was really the answer to what she was not revealing in the scene. We cannot dislike something or have resistance to something without it having some charge within us. If it weren't triggering something inside, she wouldn't have a reaction. When we use words such as "I can't relate to it," or "I hate it," or "It's stupid," those are indicators that that's why we should be doing it. Scenes themselves are all neutral in tone. It's our own loaded judgments that we bring to them that make acting hard. Same in life. If we hate someone, they're pushing a button. Our button.

Judgments be damned. Any great piece of art, music, or dance is created in-spirit without self-criticism. Picasso, while painting, wasn't thinking, "Is this okay?" I mean, come on, some of his work is really out there. The same with Salvador Dalí. If they were judging it before they created it, we never would've gotten to see it. It would have never been shared with the world. Or maybe they did judge it, but they pushed through the judgment and did it anyway. The critical factor may come later, but in the moment of inspiration, creativity seizes us to such a degree there's nothing we can do *but* create.

> *"There is a vitality, a life force, a quickening that is translated through you into action, and because there is only one of you in all time, the expression is unique. And if you block it, it will never exist through any other medium — and be lost. The world will not have it. It is not your business to determine how good it is nor how it compares with other expressions. It is your business to keep it yours clearly and directly, to keep the channel open. You do not have to believe in yourself or your work. You have to keep open and aware directly to the urges that motivate you. Keep the channel open. No artist is pleased. There is no satisfaction whatever at any time. There is only a queer, divine dissatisfaction, a blessed unrest that keeps us marching and makes us more alive than others."*
> — **Martha Graham**, *choreographer*

Life is gloriously messy. Let the palette we choose to create from be messy. Any of the higher states of consciousness — love, desire, hope, compassion — come from a non-linear, non-analytical sphere. When we're seized by one of these acts, our mind may refute it to stay in control or to keep us protected, but the actual acting out of one of these conditions is not a cognitive act.

It's inspired. It's creative. It's fearlessly living the moment. Now.

Homework, Week 7: There are three parts to this week's writing exercise. At the top of a sheet of paper, write down the question, "Who am I?" At the top of another page write, "Why am I here?" At the top of the third write, "What is my purpose?" Take one question at a time and start writing whatever comes to you. Don't judge, just write freely. Stay on each question, continuously asking the question and writing for at least three minutes. At first, you may answer in the obvious ways. "I am an artist." "I'm a woman." "I'm a dad." But as you continue writing, the answers to these questions may come from deeper places within and you might be surprised with what you end up discovering. "Why am I here?" and "What is my purpose?" may elicit the same answers. Don't worry. Just keep writing even if you repeat yourself.

After you've finished, review your lists. Maybe you see a theme. Maybe the more you write, the more your answers became less superficial and obvious and more universal, and broader. After you've reviewed your list, go to each piece of paper and circle three of your answers that most speak to you, that most excite you. You will end up with a total of nine answers. Take another piece of paper, or a blank canvas, or drawing paper, or whatever you want, and write these nine descriptions of yourself in a creative way on this new blank slate (the bigger the better, as you will be adding more to this creation).

Find a photograph of yourself that you love and glue it on the piece of paper. Think of it like an art project you created in the 5th grade. You can paint or use markers. Do it your way.

When you are finished, put your masterwork aside as you will be adding more to this next week.

"Today is not a dress rehearsal."
— Kenneth Cole

CREATIVITY

*"One of the most tragic things I know about
human nature is that all of us tend to put off
living. We are all dreaming of some magical rose
garden over the horizon — instead of the roses
blooming outside our window today."*
— Dale Carnegie

Life. It's rarely what we think it's going to be. On most days
it's better than I imagined. But that's only when I stop daydreaming (wake up!) and relinquish the control telling me it's
supposed to look a certain way. That's hard.

We spend our formative years telling ourselves what something is supposed to look like and when it's supposed to happen.
And how. But life's going to take us on its journey whether we
go along for the ride kicking and screaming or not. Sadly, what
we often end up missing (because we're so busy fighting what *is*)
is the call of creativity.

Creativity only occurs in the unknown.

We have an "ah ha!" moment. We see a film and are inspired.
We're listening to music and visualize a project. We're talking
about a world event with a friend and want to contribute to a
specific cause. All of these ideas came from something and then
the act of creativity forces us to begin. The idea, the passion, the
desire is generated within us, but to see that dream manifest we
have to start somewhere. But where?

It's a lot like a game of trust. We're being asked to move from
the world of the known ("I have a great idea!") to the world of the

unknown ("How the hell am I going to do *that?*"). Everything required to bring our idea to light will become apparent as we begin playing with our initial spark of creativity. But at the outset, we face a blank page, or an empty canvas or a barren space or a pair of tap shoes just screaming, "Jump in! Create!" We have to take a leap into the unknown, and risk failure, rejection, embarrassment, getting lost, discomfort, ridicule and oh, yes, absolute bliss. But if we don't trust the process in the leap, then the assistance — the guarantee we are looking for — can't come. As much as we don't like to do it, we are designed to take the leap. We're supposed to take the leap.

Acting is a great metaphor for illustrating how creation itself occurs in the unknown. An actor may "know" the material. He's memorized his lines, made choices and has ideas about what could or couldn't happen in a scene. But the creative inspiration comes in the total unpredictability of the moment. Something occurs, and in that unknown moment we slap our partner or start to cry or kiss him or spit on him or hug him. The inner critic wants to label the response inappropriate. "I can't do that." But in fact, it is the possibility in each moment, which contains *all* expressions of life — even those which others would call inappropriate or perverse or profane or "not nice" — that births creativity.

> *"The problem is that you bring in the critical factor before the lyric factor has had a chance to express itself."*
> — Friedrich Schiller, *poet*

And this is often the case in every art form. The singer, the poet, the writer, the musician, the athlete, the computer tech, the scientist, the teacher, the nurse, the doctor. We strike down ideas and inspirations before they have been given time to be nurtured and explored. We have this set picture of our imagined life from years ago. Any time an opportunity arises that could lead us to something different, we shout, "No!" We fear it will exclude the possibility of some other specific dream from ever happening.

I've Fought Hard For My Limitations

My close friend, Janelle, is a wonderful actress. And she makes people laugh. Hard. Like the time she wore six-inch heels to an audition, tripped on the raked stage, and slid, head first, down the embankment onto the lap of the director. Sadly, even with her head in his groin, she didn't get the part. So much for the casting couch.

Another time, she was an hour late for an audition, sending the casting director into a tizzy. As punishment, she made Janelle say her lines from behind a gigantic fern. The audition was put on tape but Janelle obediently stayed where she had been told, poking her head out from behind a leaf to say a line and then disappearing again behind its foliage. Can you say *Animal Planet?*

A number of people have encouraged her to start writing. Janelle refuses. "But I'm an actress! I'm not a writer." She has such a strong mental picture associated from a lifetime of being in show business that she believes an actress only acts. But why limit ourselves? We can do it all and every experience in our lives can awaken latent talents we never knew existed. We can be an athlete and a painter, a singer and a computer whiz, a teacher and a musician, or an actor and a writer. Anything goes. We can train for a marathon, write an opera, direct a play, and work at the local market. The only thing that limits us are our own limitations. They're limitations in the mind only.

Often, society is complicit with supporting our limited beliefs. It will mirror our own self-imposed barriers by providing constraints, labeling us as one thing only and trying to put us in a defining box. It's up to us to not allow ourselves or anyone (whether parent, spouse, teacher, sibling or well-meaning friend) to define who we are, who we can be or what we can do.

When Janelle says "no," she's cutting herself off from being the channel that she (and all of us) actually is. Perhaps the creative impulse wants to be expressed through writing because it can't be expressed in some other way. With that come possibilities: she could write a role for herself, she could discover writing fulfills her in ways that acting doesn't, and she might free herself from the pressures of having to book an acting job. She might even become more creative and act even more, because acting would no longer be the sole focus of her life.

But our mental pictures often get in our way. They create false beliefs. Janelle thinks if she writes she won't be able to act. Or worse, by starting to write, she may have to deal with a voice within her that's telling her she failed as an actress, even though she's already a success. Our contaminated thinking has such a powerful hold, it deludes us into thinking that by giving up our "dream" and comparing ourselves against society's imagined definition of "success," we've failed.

The truth is that the act of creating is far greater than the pictures we have in our heads. In fact, it's actually fulfilling the picture in a more magnificent way than the mind's miniscule interpretation of "I have to be on a TV series now," or "I can't do that because it's going to prevent me from doing this." But how do we know? We don't. Except when we're willing to take the leap and it reveals itself. But so many of us remain motionless, our feet firmly in place.

> *"And the trouble is, if you don't risk anything you risk even more."*
> — **Erica Jong**, *author*

Just Say Yes

When I moved to New York in my early 20's, I thought I'd be an actor my entire life, doing nothing else. But as I began to let go of my control of how I believed things had to look, I started expressing myself in ways that were previously unknown to me. I realized the key was to keep saying yes to what life had to offer and it will take you on a wild ride beyond your imagination.

> *"Yes is a world and in this world of yes live (skillfully curled) all worlds."*
> — e. e. cummings, *poet*

Saying yes to life ushers in a multitude of other yes possibilities that wouldn't exist if we had said no. Say yes to the waiter at your local diner who asks you out on a date. Say yes to asking your boss for a raise but you've been too scared to ask. Say yes to going to hear a lecture from someone you've never heard of before. Say yes to the voice within that encourages you to take the leap into something you've never experienced.

My God, say yes as if your life depends on it. Because it does.

Our intellect is not running the show. It only thinks it is. The ego doesn't want us to create and will do whatever it can to undermine any attempt to step into the unknown — whether that's studying acting ("I don't need a class."), or asking a girl out on a date ("She's just gonna say no."), or singing Karaoke ("That's stupid."), or taking a trip to Paris ("I can't afford it and I have no time anyway.").

To compound the problem, much of society is structured around rigid, identifiable, monetary-based models that suggest the only way of doing something is the way it's been previously done. This paradigm is difficult to overcome. Many of us live the lives we were told to live, following the paths taken by our parents and their parents.

So what do we do? We *create*. Every day. In every way. Your job is not to limit the flow. You are the instrument. You are the channel. Let source — or intelligence or energy or creative impulse or whatever you want to label it — move *through* you. We all contain creative genius within. Contain doesn't mean confine. You confine it when you plug up the opening by saying "no," or by letting fear be your first response to things. Stay plugged into the universal matrix of which we are all a part and you will connect to forces you never knew existed.

Much of our culture lives in a state of disconnect, reducing people to statistics, price-points and focus groups, numbers and trends. We exist only within the ever-important 18- to 35-year-old demographic, or the senior sector, or the minority, or the many other ways to categorize and compartmentalize people. We're no longer individuals with dreams and struggles and hopes. We're reduced to consumers, a marketing strategy, a sale. But authentic creativity comes from individual self-expression. It leads; it doesn't follow. It originates; it doesn't mimic.

Dancing To Your Own Beat

Whatever happened to that trailblazer within you? Maybe you were actually reading Shakespeare in high school English class while everyone else was reading the Cliff's Notes. Or maybe you were organizing pep rallies to improve school lunches while your classmates were more interested in choosing the homecoming king and queen. Or perhaps you were petitioning the school administration to allow girls to participate in "boys" sports.

We have to start honoring the path of our own journey and not allow other people's talked-about paths make us feel as if there's something wrong with our own. The first half of my life was all about doing things the way I felt I had to do things or I wouldn't fit in. Or be accepted. Loved. A success.

We all have something to contribute. We are of value not because of what others think of us or how others can earn a profit from us. We are of value because of what we can share of ourselves with the world. But you're not going to find that unless you're brave enough to step out onto your path and truly walk it.

Someone else's path may seem more glamorous, or more interesting, or exciting, but it's only because we aren't fully present to — and living our own — glamorous, interesting, exciting journey. We spend so much time and energy coveting what others have that we lose a sense of gratitude that we've been given our own path. We're trying to fulfill ourselves through the living of someone else's life. This tendency of human nature has been going on for thousands of years.

"It is better to do your dharma poorly than to do another man's excellently."
— **The Bhagavad Gita**

"Dharma" can be loosely translated to mean one's "truth" or "path." Humankind has been trying for centuries to not honor their individual paths. What we often do with our "grass is greener" syndrome today is the same thing that people have been doing for millennia. Everyone else's life has always seemed more exciting than our own.

The beautiful thing about waking up to our own life is that even if we've spent the last 10 years trying to jump onto another's path, as soon as we recognize that our path is our way home, then our path once again reveals itself. Talk about gratefulness. We can be lost in the forest for years — through denial, avoidance, anger, blame, or fear — and as soon as we surrender (and accept ourselves for who we are and where we are), our path is illuminated.

All The World's A Stage

Artists often feel at creative odds with themselves because of the nature of the business side of their art. Are art and commerce mutually exclusive? An actor once said to me: "My creative self and business self are vying for my attention and I don't know how to make them both happy."

I suggest this: stop compartmentalizing. What you call your business self and your creative self are actually the same entity. Find a creative way to engage in the business so that you can be fulfilled creatively while doing something that *appears* uncreative. If we bring present-moment awareness to whatever we're doing (making business calls, writing letters, sending out mailings) and are finding the joy in doing it because we're doing it our way, then that's a creative act. We aren't only creative while we're acting or writing poetry or singing a song. Live your entire life creatively. Everything we do can be a creative act if we bring a sense of self to it.

When I first moved to New York, I was auditioning for things but I just wasn't booking. (Actually, I was booking a lot of things but none of the things I wanted or thought were good enough. Can you say Diva?) So I'd whine to my friend, Brian: "I just want to act!" Finally, he'd heard enough of my pouting and shouted, "Then act!" I was flabbergasted. "What?" Didn't Brian understand how hard it was to be an actor? Obviously not, as he wasn't one. Brian nailed me, "Enough of this drama about it. If you really want to act then just act." I sputtered, "I can't."

I thought I needed someone to pay me. I needed to be doing the Broadway show. I needed to have the right agent. I needed to be getting the audition that was going to get me a meeting with Steven Spielberg. I had all these conditions surrounding what I thought acting was. They were excuses that kept me stuck and kept me in the "It's so hard being an artist" pay-off.

Busted. I wasn't able to get away with the "yes but's" anymore. "Yes, *but* they want a name. Yes, *but* it's not a paying gig. Yes, *but* it's not a network TV show. Yes, *but* I don't get my payback. Yes, *but* I'm too old. Yes, *but* they want someone else. Yes, *but* they want a famous actor. Yes, *but* I'm putting it off until I get a meeting with that agent I've always wanted to meet. Yes, *but* I'm waiting until I get new headshots." And the list goes on and on.

I'm Just Gonna Wait Another Day (Or Two) Before My Life Will Begin

What are you waiting for? Do it your own way. Create a play, make a movie, sing, paint, write, sculpt. Go out on the sidewalk of your neighborhood and perform a three-minute scene for yourself and your best friend. In order to create theatre, "at least one spectator is needed to make it a performance," says theatre director Jerzy Grotowski. All you need is one actor (yourself) and one audience member who's willing to watch you. That's it. You could snag some poor, unsuspecting shopper coming out of the Rite Aid and make him watch your street art. I once saw Queen Latifah leaving the drugstore. I could have sung for her. How liberating. It's still acting. You can create it anywhere. Right outside Starbucks or Target or Kmart or in your apartment.

Creating is creating is creating. Painting is painting is painting. Singing is singing is singing. Writing is writing is writing. Acting is acting is acting. How is embarking on a creative venture with a group of friends who share the same vision to create art better or worse than getting 10 million dollars to star in a James Cameron movie? When we enter into any creative act with consciousness and passion, integrity and authenticity, then it's all the same. It's just the ego trappings — the labels, the hubris, the fame, the recognition — that make one creative act something other, something worse, something better. But how can we compare art against art anyway? How can we judge one piece of art to be "better" than another? Art is a subjective, personal expression of one's truth.

I understand the conundrum. We need to make money to eat. And as artists we'd like to be paid for our art. And we should. Artists keep this world sane and keep connecting us to ourselves and to each other. So I do understand the economics and the necessity of it. But to understand true creativity is to also understand that the true joy in creating has nothing to do with the end results of that creative labor.

I could ask if the joy in creating in acting class is any different than the joy created in working on a movie. And we might respond, "Well, yeah! Duh, I'm getting a million dollars to act in the movie." But in truth, after we've had the creative experience, we discover that earning the money has not changed our experience of joy at all. The money isn't creating the happiness. The act of creating *in the moment* is the true source of joy and fulfillment. The money's the icing on the cake (and it may be a big fat piece of icing), but still, the *creating* is the cake.

In fact, for many people, earning the million dollars often makes things worse. They falsely equate the bliss of the creative act with the amount of money they earn and then end up wanting more money next time. "I want 20 million." Or they want the bigger house or the faster car or the hotter girlfriend or the bigger trailer or the private jet and on and on. Then you've jumped on a new hamster wheel of being unfulfilled because the monetary will never be enough. We put the end result before the act, and in so doing we're doomed to be perpetually unsatisfied. Where does it end?

I'll Enjoy This Moment Now . . . But Later

I once taught a young actress who was just starting out in the business. She was searching for an agent, a chance to get paid work, go out on auditions, and express herself. All normal desires. But she — like so many of us — was never happy with where she was. The innocence and hopefulness of that period in her life weren't celebrated because she was always looking *somewhere else* for her life to begin. She never saw those moments as being perfect; as giving birth to the exciting anticipation of the things to come. Those moments were only seen as a means to an end to take her somewhere else.

Constantly looking for that elusive happiness, which always seemed out of her reach, I told her, "Enjoy this, you'll never be here ever again." (Annoying, I know.) I knew things were going to change for her and she was going to become famous, so why not enjoy the excitement right now that made her want to be an actress in the first place?

A couple years later we spoke again as she was starring in her own TV show. All the things she'd desired had manifested. By most acting standards, she'd "made it." I thought, once again, how glorious a time for her. But strangely, the conversation was still the same as it had been years ago. The circumstances and conditions seemed to change — or had they?

Her desires had been fulfilled: she now had that great agent, was making lots of money, was a famous actress, was creatively expressed; yet although the level of her material success had changed, her inability to once again find joy in the now kept her unhappy and stuck in the never-ending cycle of unfulfilled desire. She complained she wasn't making enough money (tell that to her waiter friends who were still slinging meatloaf and potatoes), and now she was trying to get different auditions, no longer for TV but for film. "I'm done with TV," she complained.

She was still unhappy with where she was. The names and faces in her life and the amounts of money she earned had changed but it was really still her state of being wrapped up in a different package of external trappings.

We can't escape that wherever we are, there we are. The outer can never replace the inner. Ever. The true source of happiness in creating is derived not in the end result of what creating can bring us because it's insatiable, but simply in the creating itself.

"Creativity has nothing to do with any activity in particular, with painting, poetry, dancing, singing — it has nothing to do with anything in particular. Anything can be creative. It is you who brings that quality to the activity. Activity itself is neither creative nor uncreative. You can paint in an uncreative way. You can clean the floor in a creative way. You can cook in a creative way. Creativity is the quality that you bring to the activity you are doing. It is an attitude, an inner approach — how you look at things. Be a giver. Share whatsoever you can — and remember, I am not making any distinction between small things and great things. If you can smile wholeheartedly, hold someone's hand and smile, then it is a creative act, a great creative, act. Just embrace somebody to your heart and you are creative. Just look with loving eyes at somebody . . . just a loving look can change the whole world of a person."
— Osho

Wow. That's true creativity.

And something we're all capable of doing.

Homework, Week 8: Get three sheets of paper. At the top of one page write, "My Three Month Goals." Start writing. What are things you can accomplish in three months? Maybe you've been putting off going to the gym. Maybe it's time to get that project started in the next three months. Maybe you want to take a foreign language course. Or go out on a date. Or start a novel. What can you accomplish in three months if you started it today? When finished, take the second piece of paper and write under the heading, "My Six Month Goals." These may be longer-range ideas you have for yourself. They will still need to be put into action now, but don't worry about that yet. Just write whatever comes to mind that you can reasonably do in six months time. Maybe you want to start training for a marathon. Maybe in six months you will have found an agent. Maybe you'll have booked a commercial. After you have written these goals, take the last sheet of paper and write: "My One Year Goals." You know what to do. What might you have done from exactly one year from today? Take that vacation to Bali? Finished your screenplay? Bought a house? Don't worry if some of them feel a little farther away than a year. A lot can happen in a year. Don't put limitations on who you are. Just write what comes to you.

After you've completed those exercises, look over all three lists. You might notice that there is a theme — an overall underlying intention — toward a specific goal. The three-month goal might be connected to the six-month goal that is connected to the one-year goal, for example. Circle *one* goal from each of the three categories and try to circle a goal from each group that is in some way connected to the other two, if possible. You will end up with a total of three circled goals.

Now, pull out your previous artwork from last week with the descriptions of *who you are* and *why you are here* and *what is your purpose*. Somewhere on this piece of work, write down your three goals written as if you have already achieved them. In other words, "I have finished my screenplay." Or, "I am booking a commercial." Don't worry that you have more than three goals in life and on your lists. You'll still move in the direction of accomplishing all of them. But let's just focus on three for now so that you don't get overwhelmed and give up because of the sheer number of things you may begin feeling like you *have* to do.

After you've written them on your piece of artwork, display your work somewhere in your home where you can see it every day. Reminding you of why you came to this planet, who you are, what you are capable of. You don't have to do anything more with it. Just look at it and read it every day. And then go out into the world, and take action.

"I've never been particularly ambitious. I've been driven by the moment."

— Johnny Depp

WE'RE ALL HIDING AND SEEKING

"Remember who you are, because that is the most attractive thing about you. Try to allow as much of yourself as possible into what you do. That doesn't mean you play the same part or person all the time; I mean allow your spirit to come through. I used to think acting was all about putting lots of layers on top of yourself; but the older I've gotten, the more I've realized that the reason we've all become actors is because we have recognized that people are attracted to us by what we do onstage or on film. And it's not about the lines you say or the costumes you wear. It's about you — something inside of you — so never forget who you are."
— Alan Cummings

There's no such thing as a "character." There, I said it. Someone has to. Actually lots of actors are saying it more and more.

"I've never become a character. If anything, they become me. For me, acting is about turning up the parts of you that are like the character and turning down the parts that aren't. But it's all you."
— **Ryan Gosling,** *actor*

Why are we obsessed with this idea of trying to play someone we're not? It's impossible. You can't. Neither in acting nor in life. Ever. Although, we can try, but eventually, we will be found out. The truth always reveals itself. Always.

"Let the world know you as you are, not as you think you should be, because sooner or later, if you are posing, you will forget the pose, and then where are you?"
— **Fanny Brice,** *singer*

Becoming a character — becoming someone else — is a myth. In acting, "character" comes from what each individual (or collectively, the audience) projects *onto* the person playing a role. When a character appears different from what the audience *thinks* they know about the actor or a role or the story, they assume the person has transformed into that character.

In life we do the same thing. We make judgments about who we think someone is. We project our judgments onto them. "She's such a bitch," we think or, "He's an asshole," without even really knowing the person. In acting, people make the same assumptions; they think the actor is turning into a character.

Wrong.

Smoke & Mirrors

Acting is an illusion that creates a subjective response in each of us watching "the character." An actor doesn't "become a character." The "character" is *evoked out of* the human being who is playing the role. The circumstances, the story, the environment, the situation forge the character, not the other way around. Like life. When you come home from a long day at work, you don't say, "Oh, honey, I played the *character* of such an asshole!" (Well, maybe you do . . . if you're *delusional.*) Instead, you simply say, "I was such an ass today!" That's because you were. It was you. Not you playing a "character" of an ass.

So why are we always trying to *pretend* to be someone else?

Well, duh. Look at your own life. How long have you been running from who you are? We try so hard to be someone other than ourselves. We want to fit in, or to be found attractive, or liked, popular, heard, or noticed.

Think about it. How many roles do you play a day? How many leave you feeling unfulfilled, inauthentic, a fake? How many make you answer to other people and not your own voice? How many leave you exhausted and catering to everyone but your Self? How many allow you to really be?

We're taught that it's not okay to be who we are. Who you are isn't enough. Be someone else and then you'll be loved, then you'll be desirable, then you'll be famous. Lose more weight. Fix your nose. Live in a better zip code. Drive a more expensive car.

So most of us end up acting *a lot*, and worse, we're acting to ourselves. How many times have we shoved a feeling down because it was too scary to explore? I'll just put on a happy face and play that role rather than look at my addictions or unhappiness or fear.

Every time we do something we no longer want to do, we're acting. We act every time we allow someone to say something that hurts us. We act every time we believe the lies our minds tell us: we aren't beautiful or talented or powerful. We assume roles to confirm those untruths — the ditzy blonde, the nerd, the sexpot, the tough guy — legitimizing them and keeping these false models in place to forge an illusory (and yet at times, very real-feeling) identity.

Who would we be as individuals, as a community, a society, a nation, a world, if we stopped pretending? Stopped hiding? Stopped "acting?" What might we create? We'd be limitless. The irony is we already are. If only we'd stop running away from that part of ourselves we're trying to resist. We keep believing the lie: being someone else will help us tap into our genius.

The genius of character comes from being ourselves.

Awakening our artist is giving ourselves permission to fully live again. We've moved through life as one gigantic defense mechanism in order to survive. We've been rejected, or hurt, or abused. We erroneously believe we will be punished or abandoned, or considered a failure if we share our true selves. So we assume roles to protect us. To hide us. To play games. To keep from being vulnerable and taking risks. Slowly we create this armor, this defensive wall, that helps us survive, but keeps us from living.

So why do we run away from who we are and what we are feeling, pretending to be someone else?

Representing Emotion

One of my students, Jill, said, "I haven't acted with my scene partner onstage for 10 years." What? She's been busy doing substitutions directed at her partner for so long she never allowed herself to work with the feelings naturally generated by simply interacting with another human being.

In acting, a substitution is when an actor looks at the material and chooses what he or she thinks is the "appropriate" emotion for that scene and then tries to find a "trigger" from her own life to generate the feeling on stage. If the emotion doesn't come, the actor manufactures it. (And how can it come if the actor is playing an emotion on top of what she is already feeling or if she is pretending to be talking to someone other than her scene partner?) The actor doesn't trust her real feelings. Instead she recalls a similar situation from her life that she thinks generated the same emotion called for in the scene and tries to recreate the feeling.

Jill would make up feelings to play the scene instead of being in her present experience. What does this do? First, it keeps her out of the moment and from feeling her real feelings generated by the now. Dr. Phil says, "In order to feel you gotta be real." He should be teaching actors. He's right. Or the mandate could also be, "In order to be real you gotta feel."

Jill needs to get on *The Dr. Phil Show* pronto. Instead of working with the feelings that arose from being with a man onstage (or anywhere for that matter) — awkwardness, sexual vulnerability, excitement, neurosis, flirtatiousness, etc. (all the things that would perhaps be called for in the scene itself) — she instead protected herself by projecting the image of her ex-boyfriend, "Stephan," onto her partner. She pretended she was doing the love scene with Stephan.

Sadly, Stephan has been out of the picture for 10 years. *Move on, Jill!* This is not a Photoshop class. Jill denied moments as they were actually happening, instead "representing" the feelings she remembered having with Stephan and trying to add them on top of what she was saying. She "acted" feeling. And it was a lie. Later, she confided in me that she actually had a crush on her scene partner. Well, *hello*. It was obvious.

Too afraid to experience her real feelings, she opted instead to "play" those qualities she thought were needed in the scene. She couldn't generate anything real out of the substitution, which is really a fantasy. She played the past, not the present. The paradox is that she isn't that past person anymore. She has become someone new.

When I try to recall my feelings for someone, what I think happened and what actually happened have become blurry. If I were to recall a broken romance with all the pain and anguish it brought, sure, I'd find it still resides within me somewhere. But I don't have to recall a specific episode in order to work with my feelings. My experiences (including all feeling) are stored within me, and by engaging in the scene, my feelings will be automatically evoked. Now we may not always want to express them. They're too scary or unmanageable or maybe unattractive-looking. They make us feel vulnerable and exposed so we shut down. But they're there. And finding them is the real work.

Risk-Averse

It's always your life. Always. Your experiences. Your pain. Your joy. The great artist is someone who's willing to share that. This is what touches us. Whether it's a dance or a screenplay, or planting a garden or making a home-cooked meal. But the irony is that in our own lives we're programmed to be risk-averse. We avoid the exploration of Self. So how do we incorporate that which wants to be naturally evoked in our work — and that which makes us truly who we are — into our lives?

Stop denying your feelings. Onstage and off. Stop going underground with them. Stop labeling them "bad" or "painful" or "scary" or "unwanted." Just become aware of them. We don't make a big deal about the joyful things we're feeling in life, so why do we get so twisted when we start to feel things that open our wounds?

Feeling vulnerable isn't unsafe. It's just new.

When we move into new emotional territory, our old wounds may reopen and our anxieties and fears may be triggered. The feelings indicate that we're stepping into something we normally control. Newness and uncertainty aren't bad. But since we don't know how to control these new feelings, which ironically trigger old feelings stored within us at a cellular level, we continuously label them unwanted. What if we chose to simply allow them to be. That's a novel approach to living life, isn't it?

Denial — It Ain't Just A River In Egypt

In life, and in acting, when we pretend to be someone else, we miss the gift of feeling the excitement and empowerment that come out of living. We're so busy maintaining the illusion that we're someone else, we end up denying and censoring our authentic responses. As a person and an actor. Does that mean you might get aroused working on an intimate sexual scene with a partner? Yes. We may get nervous. We may feel vulnerable. We may get turned on. Our partner may excite us. So what? What's wrong with that? Why should we have to hide ourselves when someone rocks our world, even if it's just someone we work with in acting class? Why isn't it okay to tell someone they make us nervous, or we find them attractive or interesting? If we work with that, we won't have to "play" anything at all. We become the character.

I Only Want You To See The Me I Want You To See

One time in class, an actress, Sally, was exploring the role of "Alice" in a scene from the play *Closer*. She commented that she experienced the sheer degradation of playing a stripper but said that she now wanted to experience it thoroughly as Alice. "What?" I asked. "I want to totally surrender to Alice and leave Sally out of it the next time I do the scene."

Was she going to levitate out of her own body and inhabit that of Alice? That's very *The Excorcist*. Very Linda Blair. "I know how I feel about stripping," she said, "but now I want to see how Alice feels about it."

How Alice feels about it? Alice has no feelings about it because *there is no Alice!* There's only Sally. Sally decided to take her clothes off in the scene. Sally felt degraded in doing so. Sally felt naked, and vulnerable, and exposed (literally and figuratively), and in that moment of honesty and fearlessness we saw the *character* of Alice.

Sally argued that Alice wouldn't have reacted the way she did because Alice is accustomed to stripping, and she was not. She didn't think Alice would freak out. How the hell would she know? Has she gone to the Shake Shack Lounge recently with Alice? Has she watched Alice get her panties stuffed with dollar bills from rich patrons? Has she slid down a greased pole with Alice? Has she asked Alice if she's ever freaked out? That would be hard because Alice is an *imaginary* person.

Sally also struggled with her desire to "honor the play" while at the same time honoring her own experience. She kept saying, "I'd never do that but the character would."

Stop limiting what can or can't happen in a creative experience. You won't know until you create. Forget the play. Forget the playwright. Honor yourself. See what *you* discover. There's no character to honor. You are the character in her circumstances. You.

We say, "I'd never do that." Liar. Liar. Pants on fire. There are lots of things I swore I'd "never do." And now, years later in life —*Voila!* — I've done them. Stop saying, "I'd never do that." How do you know?

The playwright's writing a scene from his mind, how he envisions it. But you, the actor, are playing the role as you experience it, not how you see it. Those words on the page don't tell you how to play a scene. They give you a guideline, a suggestion, an indication of how it was played in the playwright's head and now it's up to you.

That's where actors misfire. They become interpreters rather than creators. They "play" the scene as they have read it. That's impossible. It's never going to happen that way. It's never going to be the way you hear it or see it or imagine it in your head. It should be better. And it can be better. Like life. It's never what we think it's going to be.

Think Less & Create More

Stop crippling yourself. It's as if we're runners and have bound our feet before the race. That's really not the easiest — or most joyful — way to run. So why do we hobble ourselves creatively?

Let's say I'm eating an ice cream cone that's melting. It's turning into this messy, delicious affair that I don't want to end, but at the same time I keep eating faster so it doesn't melt away. And I'm experiencing the taste, the decadence, the messiness, the sweetness, the guilt, the pleasure, the gluttony, the humidity of the summer day. All these sensations are firing at once but I'm not thinking about these things. Or rather, I may be thinking these things, but the synapses are firing so quickly I'm letting the thoughts affect my experience of eating the ice cream right now. I'm not *playing my idea* of eating an ice cream cone, or trying to recreate how I've eaten one in the past. I'm just enjoying the full experience of eating ice cream.

When one moment is complete it gives rise to the next fully creative moment; all the potential for life exists there. So how do we do that more in our creative lives? In our art? It's as simple as eating an ice cream cone.

Live it more. Enjoy it more. Think about it less.

Homework, Week 9: This week, acknowledge that when you are in certain situations you feel certain things. Don't try to deny or control your feelings or hide from them. This week, as your buttons get pushed — as they obviously will — become aware of what you normally do with the feelings.

Do you shut down by eating a bag of Doritos? Or a package of Twinkies? Do you tune out by watching some mindless TV show you've already seen twice? Do you reach for the bottle of hooch? As you witness habituated responses to the stress prompting the feelings, gently guide yourself to where the feeling is in your body. Pinpoint it. Describe it. Examine and label it. "This hurts." "I'm scared." Instead of reacting, sit with the feeling and breathe. Take 10 deep breaths and see if the feeling shifts or disappears. You may have to repeat this process a number of times before you begin to locate the feeling and really begin to understand what's happening. Ask yourself, "What is really going on here? What am I really frightened of? Or angry about?" What you discover might surprise you. What you thought you were upset about isn't what you were upset about at all.

This awareness exercise will make you cognizant that some situations in life engender certain feelings. And realize that *everyone* in one way or another feels similar feelings. Different situations may bring up different emotions for people and we have been wonderfully trained to hide certain feelings. Consequently, you think you're the only one who feels nervous or shy or inadequate in a given situation. You aren't. Barack Obama gets scared. Chaka Khan has doubts. Be gentle with yourself.

You aren't alone. There's nothing wrong with you for feeling something. It's incorrect to think that other people aren't affected by things the way you are. Don't separate yourself from others, believing the lie that you must be defective or crazy or be missing something the "perfect" people possess. We are *all* the same. Isn't that refreshing?

This week, start observing what you put into place as a reaction to triggers in your life. Write it down if you have to. "Today I got upset with my mom." When you habitually would reach for the chocolate, see what happens if this week, you breathe through it instead. Maybe you'll discover it has nothing to do with your mother at all.

"Don't ever let a soul in the world tell you that you can't be exactly who you are."
— Lady Gaga

THE JOURNEY, THE WHOLE JOURNEY, AND NOTHING BUT THE JOURNEY

"Life is a process of becoming, a combination of states we have to go through. Where people fail is that they elect a state and remain in it. This is a kind of death."
— Anais Nin

Thank You Sir; May I Have Another?

The universe gives us exactly what we're asking for. You may say, "But Tony I'm asking for a new car, and a new lover, and more money, and a new career, and it's not giving me any of those things." That's because that's not what you're actually asking for. When we're directing our energy toward what's *not* working — towards why the agent won't represent you, why all the men in your city are losers, why we can't ever seem to get ahead, or whatever the negative vibration we are sending out to the universe is — the universe can only respond accordingly. Even if we don't want those things (bad boyfriends, a non-responsive agent and zero auditions), our emphasis on those things (talking about them, obsessing about them, railing against them, and complaining about them to friends) and the general negative vibration attached to them is saying to the universe, "More of this stuff that isn't working please."

To understand this phenomenon further, let's take a look at the nature of desire and why we desire the things we do. The things we desire — the new pair of shoes, the hot girlfriend, the two-story house or record deal — are all the things that we think will bring fulfillment and happiness.

Generally, we say, "If I had those things, then I'd be happy," but first we have to be happy before the universe can give us the things we desire. In an energy-based universe, we can't put the chicken before the egg. We have to change our feeling first and then life will begin to take shape supporting that emotional offering.

This is partly because the things we desire that we *think* will bring us happiness . . . (wait for it) . . . won't. *What?* I know you're thinking, "Tony's nuts! I'm happy when I'm sipping a mai-tai on a beach in Waikiki. I'm happy with my new plasma screen TV." Well, yes, the beach and the mai tai and lots of other things will bring satisfaction and momentary pleasure, sure, but lasting joy never comes through the transitory things we do (or do not) acquire or amass or do. Everything in this world is temporal, which in itself creates a non-lasting effect. Eventually, the things we desire we'll lose, or grow tired of, or want something instead of — and because they're temporary, they will never sustain lasting happiness. We outgrow the toys we once loved. We lose touch with old friends. We trade things in for upgrades. But the universe itself — and our own internal state of happiness — is not externally referenced, because it's not temporal.

Things don't make us happy, even though we erroneously think they do. Look at someone who gets married and divorced, then married and divorced. "And here I thought marriage would make me happy." Or someone gets their dream car and then wants another, bigger car. Or someone who signs with a big talent agency and then wants to be with an even more powerful company. Or someone who's acting on TV and then wants to do movies.

There's nothing wrong with desiring things. As I said earlier, the nature of desire is inherent to being human. But thinking that the fulfillment of these things is the fountain of happiness that is eluding us — *is* the illusion. And it keeps postponing us from living and experiencing happiness now.

The Anatomy Of Desire

Our real evolution in life does not occur through the accomplishing of things or acquiring stuff. If the fulfillment of our desires permanently satiated us — we'd never evolve. Can you imagine if I got a new car because that's what I desired and then never wanted anything ever again? "Hey Tony let's go see this new movie." "No," I say, "I just got my new car. I will never desire anything ever again." What? (Look at the planet in Darwinian terms. It's been "desiring" — evolving — since the days of bacteria and microbes were the only living forms on our planet some three and a half billion years ago.)

The world and all the myriad expressions of life would simply stop existing if we stopped desiring. The nature of the universe (and all it contains) has an encoded evolutionary DNA. Its purpose? To fulfill nature's desire to expand and express the ever-more complex creations of life. Desire calls forth new life, new ideas, new forms, new possibility for diversity.

In our own lives, the desiring of things is our true Self's way of knowing and expressing itself. The things we want can't bring lasting happiness but they can compliment our inherent natural state of joy. In other words, the things we want are an example of Self knowing *itself* through the spontaneous fulfillment of those desires. We came to this planet to be powerful, to be fully expressed, joyful, infinitely creative, to love. Any fulfillment of a desire that evokes these qualities is an example of aligning with our spirit or who we really are — our natural state.

Our natural state is not that of lethargy or sadness, or of feeling badly, guilty, or shameful. It's not feeling fearful that there isn't enough or that we don't count. Think about it. When we feel those things, doesn't it suck? That's because it's antithetical to who we are and a deeper part of us knows this. To feel happier we have to get in touch with that part of ourselves that is already bliss. That is already joyful, all-knowing and fully expressed.

Love, hope, faith, compassion are not qualities that can be taught. Yet no one denies they exist in the world. I can't point to something and say this is what love is, this is what it looks like, and now I'm going to break it down conceptually and define it. Because love — and any of the higher states of emotional expression — transcends theory. Try to describe love. Do words capture and express the *feeling* of love? Love transcends words.

Whip Me, Beat Me, Slap Me

When I was in college, I'd try to emulate all the other thespians who were quite dramatic in their efforts to "get it right." "Oh, if I don't really struggle and create my character arc and the through-line and a ten-page character history and work out my character's spine and his inner animal and my intentions on each line, if I don't *suffer* for my craft, I must not be learning anything. It can't really be easy."

There's nothing virtuous about struggling except that our ego gets the most amazing stroking by people who acknowledge how hard we worked. It goes against the laws of nature. There isn't a lot of struggle in nature. Trees grow, flowers bloom, tadpoles become frogs. And even in the most inhospitable of climates, nature just does its thing. It's only when man interferes with what occurs naturally, that the balance and ease of things begins to become contaminated.

Why do we make it so hard for ourselves? Why do we like pain? 'Cause we're sadomasochistic. *Stop it, right now!* We're taught to believe that if we're not really working hard we must not be learning. When I mean work hard, I'm talking about confusing going after our goals in life and overcoming challenges — which is necessary and a natural part of process — with the mental abuse we heap on ourselves, which isn't necessary or productive. We associate setbacks and obstacles with negativity, pain, confusion, torment, fear, and resistance in relation to what we want to be doing: creating. We think all of that stuff (i.e. *drama*) is necessary to create.

One of my students commented on how much joy one of his fellow classmates has in her work and couldn't understand why acting seemed to come so easy for her. Well, it *is* easy when we're creating from that joyful, playful, effortless space. The harder we make something, the harder it becomes. But if we get out of our own way, something bigger can work through us with ease.

Einstein commented on how many of his discoveries occurred when he surrendered the critical mind and everything it was trying to control. He'd go for a walk when he was stuck on some theory and then come back an hour later and the answer to his most perplexing questions would appear. Effortlessly.

It's Good . . . No . . . It's Bad!

When I use the words "good" or "bad," or "negative" or "positive," I am not labeling experiences as either "good" or "bad." Everything is neutral in effect, and becomes labeled "good" or "bad" based on judgments and moral categorizing of the situation. Shakespeare's Hamlet said, "There is nothing either good or bad, but thinking makes it so." In other words, we ascribe a judgment to life experiences based on our personal views, likes, dislikes, desires, expectations — in short, our thinking.

When something occurs contrary to our liking or in opposition to what we think should be happening, we call these experiences "bad." But we often interpret life from a very limited perspective. What we might call "bad" today may be revealed later to have been an absolutely necessary and essential experience in our growth. What we were quick to judge as a negative has revealed itself to be something else completely.

It's been said events that occur in our realities do not cause suffering, but it is our stories about these events that do. That is, our judgments, labels, and beliefs that they shouldn't be happening. What if we were less judgmental of all events occurring in our lives? We're not at the finish line yet. Stop trying to call the race a victory or a loss until the entire race has been run.

Your Energetic DNA

Pure potential energy, which is the energy that births a star or grows a tree, is the same energy field within you. Ever notice that all these things in nature are just doing their thing? The tree is "treeing," the star is "starring." And Tony is "Tony-ing" according to my unconscious and conscious transmitters.

A weed is a great example of an organism fulfilling its universal potential to grow. The weed doesn't get in its own way of its intention to thrive. It just grows, no matter what. I recently saw this phenomenon first-hand. A weed grew out of a crack in the sidewalk near my acting studio. It was very tall, straining toward the sunlight and pushing its way through the cement. All around it was a sea of asphalt, no other plant life in sight. This weed's seed had been deposited in the most unlikely of places but its nature — its DNA — didn't care that it was in a botanical jungle or cement jungle — it was simply fulfilling its intention to grow. We're like this. We just get in our own way. We become our own cement.

We've been given this wonderful capacity to think (we have this amazing communication between the left and right hemispheres of our brain) but unfortunately, the mind (i.e. the left brain) — when used incorrectly — gets in the way of our potential to realize our intent. Like the weed, I just want to manifest the pure potential of Tony. But somewhere along the line, my thinking gets in the way, and my manifesting becomes almost haphazard. I have doubts and fears and negative thoughts and obsessive patterns that sabotage me from the pure potential energy that I am.

The tree fulfills its intent to produce healthy bark, strong roots, and chlorophyll-producing leaves. I'm similarly encoded to fulfill my intent: to joyfully, abundantly, uninhibitedly create. But unlike the tree, I'm making the un-manifest the manifest by what I'm consciously emoting. And the vibration is being sent through the thoughts I think and the feelings I hold regarding a certain subject. In other words, the tree is manifesting its potential unencumbered because it doesn't possess a consciousness. The tree doesn't know it's a tree. A tree has intelligence (the intelligence to grow) but it doesn't *know* that it has intelligence. It just does what it's engineered to do.

We human beings, on the other hand, get in our own way because we know we have intelligence. We're too damn smart for our own good.

Now Or Never

We need to act as if we already have what we desire because, in actuality, we do. In the moment that we intend something, it's here in this universe. If it weren't, we couldn't think of it. We couldn't think of what we desired if it weren't already here. The birthing of a thought comes from an idea. The resources have already been supplied. But because of our identification with time, we often get stuck. We either give up or get upset when the thing we desire hasn't revealed itself to us within our construct of time; two weeks from today or a year from now. We're never going to experience this thing in the field of time anyway, but we let "time" determine our happiness.

What does the field of time mean? Think of it as a construct. Say your parents are coming to visit you one week from today. (You better clean that house!) When they arrive, you're experiencing their arrival *now*. There is no field of experience outside of the present moment, but because of our reliance on time (as a construct) and our identification with it, we are often not even aware of the eternal field beyond the social construct of time. Pure consciousness (which is our essential nature) doesn't exist in time. It transcends time. It's now. The field of time may say it is 4:30 P.M., Tuesday afternoon, when your parents arrive. But that experience, indeed all experiences of life, exist in the eternal field called now. There will never be a time when we aren't experiencing something in the now — whether it is 4:30 P.M. on a Tuesday or three weeks from today at midnight.

As you're reading this, three weeks from today at midnight is the future. But when we experience that moment it will be *now*. We use time as a demarcation of sorts to structure our lives, to go to the store, and run to the gym, and pick up our parents at the airport. But time is an illusion.

"Time is the ultimate unreality that is solely a practical operating aid in the mental circuitry of some living organisms, to help with specific functioning activities."
— Robert Lanza, *physicist*

Think about it. Man's observation of (and reliability on) nature's recurring events (the affects of tides, the change of seasons, the phases of the moon, to name a few) were employed as ideas to keep track of time. Then as a society emerged, time was identified for political and religious and economic reasons. It was used for specific needs and imposed on people.

So is time real? Who decided that there were only going to be 12 months in a year? Why not 14 months? 18? And why is each month around 30 days long? Who structured how long a month should be? And why is a day 24 hours? Why is lunchtime at noon? Why do we work 40 hours and show up at our jobs Monday through Friday? And what is a Monday anyway?

> *"The experience of time that anyone has at any particular moment in history is an invention. It is neither God-given nor physics-given and it is very much a social construct that is built both out of the science and technology of that culture. ...Laying 24 hours on top of {a day} is the social construct. What is 1:17 {P.M.}? That number wouldn't have even made sense 500 or 1,000 years ago."*
> — Adam Frank, *physicist*

These distinctions that are used to carve out our existence and make businesses run and keep things on schedule and give us order and control are still at the mercy of one truth that transcends time. There is only going to be the "eternal now" and everything that we think of as "time" sits within it.

The Last Actor Standing

Earlier, when I talked about acting as if we already have that thing we want, we're expressing our power of intention. Let's say we've set forth the intention of creating a relationship. If we want a girlfriend, as soon as we desire her, as soon as we have put forth a clear intention for that to happen, the *possibility* for this experience to occur and the myriad permutations in which it can unfold have been orchestrated by the universe. But our inner conflicts, doubts, and fears keep us from her. Just because she hasn't been revealed to us yet, we lose hope. We're stuck on the way the scenario looks. And we use "time" as a destructive force.

The outer circumstances haven't yet changed; the obstacles are still there. It hasn't happened "yet" according to what we think is reasonable "time," so we give up. We basically cauterize our good intentions. We neutralize them, because we've blocked our intention of wanting a girlfriend with, "I'm ugly, I can't get a date, why would anyone want to go out with me? Where is she? It's never going to happen." So our negativity becomes a repelling force. So, five minutes before bumping into her at a Starbucks, we miss her, like trains running on opposite tracks.

Our own feelings of unworthiness keep us from our desires. The challenge of life is to not become dismayed by the way it "looks." We don't want to give up before the "girlfriend" materializes.

A student gave me a great acting analogy for this concept. She thinks success in Hollywood (or anywhere for that matter) comes to the person who can stay standing in the room the longest. Take 10 actresses trying to make it in Hollywood facing equal obstacles. Over time, the things they want to see happen — book a television series or a commercial, get an agent — don't happen. They haven't yet realized these desires, so one actress stops, then another one drops out, and another actress moves to Idaho. Eventually, there's only one woman left standing. She becomes the one we call a "success" because the other women gave up long before the evidence of success appeared. If you planted a seed, you wouldn't dig it up every day to see if it had yet sprouted roots, would you?

Remember those green bean seeds planted in middle school as part of a science project? The poor things would never have grown if we kept digging to see if something was happening. Life's like that.

Stop being Veruca Salt from *Willy Wonka & The Chocolate Factory* ("I want my Oompa Loompa now, Daddy!"). When we don't get what we want right away — as soon as we've demanded something — we give up. We have to retrain our thinking. We have to reprogram our own inner system and not be affected by everything we see outside of us. It can be hard when we live in a society that's microwaveable by its very nature. Everything we want seems to be ready in five minutes or less, from our instant oatmeal to instant credit. When we don't immediately get the more important things we desire it can be disconcerting. But with patience and certainty, we can learn how to trust in the process of our own lives unfolding according to their nature.

Attention And Intention

So how do we begin to become more conscious of what we're manifesting in life? The answer lies in our attention and intention. Whatever we put our *attention* on increases. *Intention* is the energy that transforms and crystallizes. It's the seed that's been planted and contains within it the potential to germinate. The intention is for the future but it is created in the present and out of the object of our awareness. It's the wiring plugged into our hard drive. Our thoughts are the hard drive, and our intentions are the wiring.

> *"Your intent is for the future but your attention is in the present. As long as your attention is in the present, then your intent for the future will manifest because the future is created in the present."*
> — Deepak Chopra, *physician*

If we become more mindful of what we're putting our focus on right now, and shift the energy and thoughts from uncertainty, doubt and fear to happiness, peace, and joyful expectation, then our intention for the future is paving the way for circumstances and events that will reinforce joy, happiness and peace. Because truly, what everyone is intending for themselves is, as I mentioned earlier, something they think (in having) will make them feel happier or more fulfilled or at peace. Once you get there you realize those things (the new boat, the Prada shoes) aren't it, but the *feeling* part is. So intend for improved feeling. Don't intend for stuff.

But It Feels Good To Feel Bad, Damn It!

Why is it so much easier to blame the world? Because we're invested in our suffering. There's a pay-off in talking about how we can't get a boyfriend or that new job or an agent. Or get that script sold. Or get hired. Or get into shape. Because in reality, getting what we truly want forces us to step up to a new level of accountability. This may trigger issues of self-worth, self-esteem, and what we think we deserve in life. It's safer and easier to keep promoting this false myth of our inability to get what we want and make it be about "outside" forces — whether a friend, lover, parent, enemy or God — rather than looking at our own hand in creating our lives. We are very, very good actors in life in the role of "playing the victim." Our problems keep us rooted to the known. They keep us safe. If we didn't complain, we wouldn't know who we were.

All "problems" in life (and their requisite pain, suffering, anger, outrage, depression) come from the denial of what *is* happening. Our egos tell us what should be happening and fervently deny what *is*. I *should* be rich. I *should* have a boyfriend. I *should* have a huge career by age 30. Or, I *shouldn't* still be waiting tables. I *shouldn't* be sick. I *shouldn't* have blown that audition. When did we allow our ego to become the boss? Our steadfast refusal to accept what *is* in life (reality) by saying it *should* be something other when it isn't — is *the* cause of our suffering.

Removing suffering is acceptance. It is the surrendering to the "is" of life and working with how to make something *other* occur. The surrender to what *is* empowers us to take action and change our circumstances. It's not about giving up. It's about acceptance that we can transform the situation into something that serves us and does not keep us in resistance. There's a lesson in everything. Feel whatever it is that's going on. When you've had enough, you'll drop it. It's just a choice away.

Homework, Week 10: This week's homework is all about restoring balance and looking at areas of our lives that require us to do a little tender gardening. Take a piece of paper and draw a large circle and then split the circle into four separate quadrants. Like a pie cut into four very large slices. On the outside of one of the quadrants, write the heading: "Career." On the second quadrant, write "Love & Relationships." On the third, write "Spirit & Well-Being." On the last section, write "Hobbies."

Now within each quadrant, write down what it is you are specifically doing to fulfill that area of your life. For example, in the quadrant of "Spirit & Well-Being" maybe you write down that you are doing yoga and going on hikes and reading inspiring books and meditating every day for five minutes (!) and taking more time for yourself. Or maybe you write nothing. The same goes for "Hobbies." What do you do outside of work? Or maybe you have a 9-to-5 job that is taking up a lot of your time, and what you write in your "Hobbies" section is what you actually want to be doing with your life: painting, writing, sculpting.

For your "Career" section, write down what you are doing every day to help move your artistic career forward. Taking class and going to networking functions and asking for help (that's a novel idea). And in your "Relationship" section, write down what you are doing to fulfill yourself in that area.

After you have finished writing whatever comes to mind in each section, observe which quadrant is emptiest. Which area of your life requires a little bit of tender loving care?

This week, you're going to actually take the steps to fill the quadrant that is emptiest. If you have zero activity in "Relationships" then you have to ask someone out on a date. If you have no "Hobbies" listed, it's time you found something to do besides sitting around watching TV. If you have no idea what "Spirit" even is, maybe it's time for you to figure it out. Maybe take a meditation class? A yoga class? Spend some time in nature? And if you say you're a painter but there's nothing happening in your "Career" quadrant, then you better examine why that is.

It may be a little scary at first, but you need to step out into the world and jump-start areas of your life that aren't activated. Make something happen. Why is that area of your life as barren as a desert? Acknowledge your fears and the resistance you have in regards to that subject matter and then get out of your own way and go do something.

We are striving for balance through all of the exercises in this book. A balance that will make us feel more energized, hopeful, alive, and creative. Balance that will help restore our joy for living.

"Security is mostly a superstition. It does not exist in nature, nor do the children of men as a whole experience it. Avoiding danger is no safer in the long run than outright exposure. Life is either a daring adventure or nothing."

— Helen Keller

LIVING IN "THE ZONE"

*"Living is a form of not being sure, not knowing
what's next or how. The moment you know how,
you begin to die a little. The artist never entirely
knows. We guess. We may be wrong, but we take
leap after leap in the dark."*
— Agnes de Mille

"Acting is a mystery."
— Meryl Streep

But is it really? Any great teaching embraces at its core a universal truth that the nature of all experiences in this world is paradoxical. For example, sometimes when I'm talking to my students they get upset because a comment I may make one week is completely contrary to a point I made the week prior. "But Tony, you said last week I was being too angry. Now you're saying I'm not angry enough!" (Partly this is so because what was true the week before might no longer be valid in the present moment if we are relating differently to the situation and person.) But the important thing here is that there are no absolutes. I am *both* one thing *and* the other at the same time. I can be fiercely angry *and* compassionate. When I was a kid, my mom would get angry if I played in the middle of the street and would reprimand me, but she did it out of love.

Another example: I'm a teacher while at the same time I'm a student. We often compartmentalize ourselves. I'm a director or actor or father or brother or American — these are the "roles" I play in my life; the "parts" I know myself to be. But I'm not only the part. I'm also the whole. I'm bigger than the parts themselves. And yet I forget that I'm the whole when I'm playing the part because we get so caught up in the "roles" we play and lose connection to a greater sense of Self.

So life is paradoxical by nature. It is a mystery and yet it is known. Or we could say how to access the mystery can be known. The mystery is that the urge to create — that desire — comes from a deep, resonant, non-cerebral place within. Suddenly, hidden things become revealed. We let go and access our true nature. Simultaneously our thinking, cognitive mind gets out of the way. We open to something bigger than ourselves, allowing it to move through us.

Peak Experiences

Any "peak experience" contains within it an element of the mysterious. We're watching a film and feel a personal connection to the story and begin to sob. We're making love to our beloved and feel a suspension of time and space, seeing our reflection in our partner's eyes. We go dancing and are transported by the music's beat and rhythm and lose ourselves to this greater flow.

Athletes talk about this experience when they're in "the zone." All of the technical elements of their training come together, and they perform effortlessly, almost magically. Many people feel it while stimulated under the influence of drugs ("Hugs not drugs" is my motto) because they're uninhibited and no longer identify with their critical mind. These peak experiences are moments when we — living in the field of time — encounter timelessness. That's what being "in the zone" is. That's what timelessness feels like. They are the experiences of the eternal right here and right now.

When we're "in the zone" we're not aware of "time." The concept of time (and all its relative cognitive associations) shuts out the eternal. We can't be "in the zone" when we're clockwatching. (Seriously, have you ever felt "in the zone" while at work, waiting for 5:00 P.M. to arrive as the clock appears to excruciatingly click slower than anything you can imagine? Probably not.) Eternalness, however, is beyond time. When we lose ourselves in the moment in a fulfilling activity or in the joy of self-expression or intimacy or physical feats, we connect to the eternal, quantum energy that transcends thoughts and the human body.

Runners . . . To Your Marks

One of my fondest childhood memories is also, coincidentally, one of these "zone" moments. I was in the 8th grade and once again it involved my sister, Angie.

Unlike a couple years earlier during my gymnastics/cheerleading phase, I think Angie was now tired of always having to spend her free time as my coach (or class bodyguard). Now in high school and more interested in boys than having to baby-sit her bratty kid brother, she agreed to help me with my hurdling technique. Or my parents forced her. To this day, I'm not quite sure which it was.

Whatever the case, Angie was a star track athlete and I was pretty fast, too (maybe it was the speed I gained running away from kids who threatened to beat me up, which happened a lot). I decided to run hurdles. I wasn't very tall (which was probably a reason I *shouldn't* have hurdled), but it was fun to win and I always liked the feeling of my body taking flight as I cleared each obstacle. Plus, it seemed more glamorous than simply running. By the 8th grade I already loved glamour.

At 15, I was the fastest hurdler on the Kesling Komets track team and my arch rival from the Boston Bruins was the six-foot tall, Bill Binder. He constantly nipped me at the finish tape and one day I realized he did this by taking three steps between each hurdle. I was taking four.

Enter Angie. We worked every day after my regular practice and on weekends. What the hell was my real coach doing? In those days they pretty much left us to fend for ourselves. So Angie stepped in and taught me to elongate my stride and trust that I had enough speed to take me to the next hurdle with fewer steps in between. I learned the biggest hurdle wasn't the actual metal obstacle but the *mental* one. I didn't think I could run with so few steps between each hurdle and jump over them without falling flat on my face.

One day at the Kesling-Boston dual meet championships, with Angie at the starting line encouraging me to *just do it* (long before Nike ever invented that phrase, by the way), I decided I *could* get over those hurdles in three steps and I *could* beat that cocky Bill Binder who always tried to psyche me out by spitting in my lane. Rude. Until that point, I'd never successfully gotten over more than three or four hurdles with three steps in between. My sister would threaten to raise the hurdle bar higher if I didn't at least try. That was a terrifying threat to a boy who was just entering puberty and wanted to protect his family jewels.

On that day there were 10 hurdles to clear. The last thing I remember was standing at the starting line, looking down my lane at the rows of hurdles and thinking, "What have I done?" Bang! The gun went off. Nirvana. Bliss. I went flying. All the weeks of Angie absent-mindedly watching me out of the corner of her eye while flirting with senior superstar quarterback Steve Jenkins, and yelling insults at me every time I crashed into a hurdle, faded to a blur. I was a machine. The hurdles flew by.

Bill, in his red Boston Bruins jersey, was nowhere to be seen. Did I false start? Was this a dream? Was I running in my underwear, causing everyone else to stop because I looked ridiculous?

Could running over these obstacles really be this easy? Was I three-stepping? I wasn't even counting. Was I actually smiling as I ran across the finish line first? Had I just had my very own *Chariots of Fire* moment that seemed to be filmed in slow mo?

I won that day in a new meet record for the 100-meter hurdles. I had no idea what happened. It was over in a flash and I don't remember counting any steps. I guess I stopped thinking and something took over and ran *me* over those 10 hurdles. And yet I felt in control while also free. There and yet *not there*. I three-stepped my way so far ahead of Mr. Binder, he crashed on the eighth hurdle, apparently because he wasn't used to seeing his competitor's ass in front of him.

My sister high-fived me, confirming that I did, indeed, three-step between each hurdle and it was, therefore, *not* a hallucination, and then ran over to the star of the baseball team, Tom Johnston, who took her behind the bleachers to smoke a cigarette and make out. I collected my first-place blue ribbon and congratulated Bill, who was still reeling from his first-ever defeat. *Buh-bye.*

I ran the hurdle race a few more times that spring. I was never able to three-step the entire race again. From that day on, Bill Binder remained undefeated in every hurdle race he entered through the 10th grade. I switched to running the 100-meter dash instead.

But My Baggage Hasn't Yet Arrived!

"Peak experiences are when we become attuned through awareness to our own harmony with nature."
— Abraham Maslow, *sociologist*

We're in full form. Both timeless and living in the world of time. The Japanese have a similar term called *mono no aware* (pronounced *moh-noh-noh, ah-wah-ray*), which loosely means, the realization of the transitory nature of reality. In a peak moment of bliss we're also aware of its transitory nature. It's a paradoxical realization: a joy in this *now* moment, while at the same time an appreciation for the awareness that this exact moment will be forever gone, cannot be held, will never be repeated again.

When we're fully present in the moment, the past has never existed and the future has yet to be born. In other words, associations with who we were (our past) and all the baggage of past experiences, or our fantasies and projections (our future) are not distracting us from living this moment of now. We generally aren't present in life because we're reminiscing about the past or planning ahead for a preferred future. In a peak experience, we have the awareness that all that exists is what we're living moment-to-moment. We're fully expressed. Not thinking, just being. For artists of any kind, it means being present with whatever is going on, whatever is welling up from deep within, and then expressing that truth through the art. This is that mysterious place that Meryl Streep is talking about, because it's not coming from the linear, reasoning mind.

For many people, being "in the zone," becomes the first experience of total surrender, not only in their work but in their life. It's an alchemical process because we are surrendering to the thrill of chance (and as we know the moment contains nothing *but* chance) and the changeability that comes with real connection with ourselves and another human being.

Surrender Dorothy

I once had a student who refused to listen in his work. For more than a year he struggled and would check out when he was in a scene and say lines as if reciting them from memory. I kept pushing him to react, but because his listening was completely shut down it was nearly impossible.

Finally, he had a "light bulb" moment, becoming aware of how *not* present he was. (And the moment we realize we aren't present, we become present.) He confided that in his family, men aren't allowed to express deep emotion, except anger. Being Latin, he was taught that, culturally, men who react emotionally were considered sissies or weak. He'd be humiliated for exhibiting these feelings. He realized he wasn't listening in his scene work because listening would force him to feel things that he was conditioned not to feel. Listening was his way in, but he didn't want to go in because going in meant dealing with feelings that were either unfamiliar, or unsafe, or inappropriate — in fact, terrifying.

Not feeling is *not* okay. But he never realized this. He wasn't aware that there was something missing in his life — the expression of natural human feelings.

Sometimes, I'll have a student who is so in the moment that his or her self-expression is always mysterious, always unpredictable. Often classmates will say, "Well that's easy for her, she's so free." But her ability to experience freedom in her work isn't any more or less than any other person's. We're all hard-wired to self-express in uniquely individual ways. She just chooses the path of least resistance in her ability to create. It's called surrender.

Many of us have so much resistance around letting go in our work and showing our true feelings in life, that we aren't even available to those intuitive moments moving through us. Consequently, when we see someone else doing it we say, "That's easy for her." And that's okay if we do. Eventually, we can do it, too.

The hard part, as one of my students once asked, "How do we live in this moment-to-moment experience *in life?* It's easy to do in a 10-minute scene in class but not always so easy to translate to our everyday lives."

So how do we do it? Moment-to-moment.

Homework, Week 11: Write your obituary. Don't get freaked out here. Use this exercise as an opportunity to show you how much of your life you *aren't* living. Years ago, I read this inspiring woman's blog (Roz Savage) who was in a dead-end job and felt her life's purpose was being wasted. Needing to make a change, she wrote two obituaries for herself and then realized if she were to leave the planet today, she hadn't done any of the things she wanted to do in life. So she quit her job, bought a boat and rowed across the Atlantic because that's what she'd always wanted to do. Unbelievable.

So this is an exercise to see how often we hold ourselves back from living the life we deeply desire. Write two obituaries. The first one is an obituary that will be read at your funeral tomorrow. That's right. If you were to depart this world tomorrow and could hear what is being said about you at your own wake, then write it. Write down who you think you will be remembered as and what you will be remembered for if you were to leave tomorrow. Did you do the things you wished to do? Were you an inspiration? Were you living your dreams? Be honest. Don't hold back. Write it as you have lived it.

After you have written it, put it aside and get out a new piece of paper. Now write the obituary you wish to have read when you die — but it's the obituary of the life you truly lived. The life of possibility. Write down all the things you've ever dreamed of doing. If you always wanted to go to Europe, but still haven't done so, write in your new obituary what you experienced in Europe and how it changed your life. Write about your swimming across the English

Channel if that's what you've always wanted to do. Write about your adopting two children from an impoverished country. Write about your loves and your successes and your artistic victories. Write about the charities you started and the people you've helped. Write about the people you met and the lives you've changed. When you are done, compare the two. Which is a life more lived? Which is a life filled with passion and adventure and romance and victories and peace of mind?

The third part of the homework — since you aren't yet dead — is to now live this obituary backwards. "What?" Well, since you're still alive (yippee!) you now have a second chance (so to speak) in living these things. What are you waiting for? Do you want your obituary to read like the first or second version? This week, start putting into motion one of the things you keep postponing in your life. If it was something you wrote in your second obituary, then it means you accomplished it. So what's it going to take for you to go out and do it? Leave nothing to chance. Live the life you intended to live. If you want to live the life you created for yourself in that second obituary, it's going to require you stepping out of your comfort zone.

You can do it.

"If you're not scared stepping into something then you're not doing the right thing."
— Sandra Bullock

DO IT! THEN FIX LATER

*"If you're looking for your path, you're already
on it."*
— Anonymous

The more you sit around thinking about doing something, you're screwed. We think about making that phone call to someone who can help us, starting that business we've been dreaming about, taking a writing course, going to Spain. And the more we think, the less we do. All sorts of reasons, excuses, rationalizations, arguments (read: fears) invade and pollute the mind with how this isn't possible. We listen to those lies and end up retreating from life's moment-to-moment experiencing and get stuck in the cerebral and judgmental. We get trapped asking ourselves, "What if . . ." So, what originated as an exciting, inspired idea eventually becomes an after-thought. We do nothing. We let the dream die.

"Until one is committed there is hesitancy, the chance to draw back, always ineffectiveness. Concerning all acts of initiative (and creation), there is one elemental truth the ignorance of which kills countless ideas and splendid plans: that the moment one definitely commits oneself then Providence moves too. All sorts of things occur to help one that would never otherwise have occurred. A whole stream of events issues from the decision raising in one's favor all manner of

unforeseen incidents and meetings and material assistance which no man could have dreamt would come his way. I have learned a deep respect for one of Goethe's couplets: 'Whatever you can do or dream you can, begin it. Boldness has genius, power, and magic in it.' Begin it now."
— **W.H. Murray,** *mountaineer*

Let's say we're trying to find an agent and haven't had any luck. Suddenly, we're seized by this great idea to start calling talent agencies and invite them to come see our work in class. That's a great idea. What happens? We share the idea with a friend. He says, "I don't think an agent would be interested but go for it, dude!" Then we start to think. Uh oh. We obsess, "My friend's right, they're just going to say 'no.'" or "What if they hang up on me?" or "The assistant is never going to put me through to an actual agent." The comedian, Jerry Lewis, calls the doubts other people place into our heads "little drops of poison." They stop us in our tracks.

Before we know it, we've gone from an inspired idea to *thoughts* about the idea to *thoughts* about *thoughts* about *thoughts* about that original idea. We're no longer connected to the original feeling of excitement and hopefulness that were engendered when we first thought it. We're screwed.

This is what Murray was referring to when he said, "Begin it now." He didn't say think about it. He didn't say obsess about it. He didn't say question it and attempt it later. He didn't say put it aside and ask for the opinions of other people. He didn't say sleep on it and re-examine it tomorrow. He said do it. *Now.*

He was aware of how powerful the movement is from the imaginative realm into the physical realm of creativity. But we have to take action. We have to begin it. And *any* kind of action is better than sitting around and coming up with all the reasons why something won't work. Even if what we were hoping doesn't manifest; by playing in the realm of possibility, we create forces that present something else to us. New creativity becomes available, new ideas and new information are accessed that may lead to something even better than the original idea. But we have to act on it.

Part of our dilemma in our culture is that we try to conform to the images we're being fed through the media. We think we have to be like that person in order to get a job or book a commercial or secure an agent or write a novel or sell a painting or be a success. We do what we think we're supposed to do as opposed to following our own instincts and creative inquiry.

I Need It. Well . . . I Don't Need It, But I Want It. Well . . . I Don't Want It, But I Have To Have It!

All of us are guilty of letting the culture (or rather the media's shaping of the culture) define and tell us what's sexy, or desirable, or attractive, or beautiful, or important, or successful. "I need to look like 'her' in order to be desirable. I need to lose 10 pounds because everyone else is a size two. I need to wear 'these clothes' because I'm not hip if I don't." We don't need these things they're trying to sell but the message is that if I wear these pants or drive this car or party at this hotel, "I'll find true love or success or friends or happiness or be a part of the 'in' crowd. Finally my life will really begin. If I just buy these sunglasses or drink this cola, my life will have meaning. My life will be as glamorous as that celebrity's life is."

"The whole world would be better off if people thought for themselves and trusted themselves instead of doing what television commercials tell them to do or thinking in whatever way the media tells them to think."
— Bode Miller, *Olympic skier*

We constantly compare ourselves to a fictionalized ideal. "I don't look like the hot leading man, so I must not be masculine enough." "I don't exude that sexiness which famous film actresses seem to have so I'm never going to get work." We begin to manufacture these incorrectly perceived "missing" qualities, comparing ourselves to Hollywood stars and tabloid celebrities. But this prevents us from revealing our true selves. So we start "acting." We become people we aren't. We ignore our own hidden aspects of who we are — our sexiness, vulnerability, passion — and put in their place this artificial mask, measuring ourselves against this unreal standard that is created out of the illusion of the media machine.

Outwardly everything looks "good." We're "too cool for school," or we act superhero tough, or put up defensive walls, but inside we're dying — we're shriveling up and wanting to be seen and heard. But we manufacture this illusion so that we appear like all the other people who seem to have it all together. They're so glamorous. Their lives are magical. They have it all. So what if they end up in jail? We think, "I have to act that way in order to have what they have." The irony here is that every human being on the planet is feeling the same thing. The house we buy or the jeep we drive or designer clothes we wear don't immunize us from the insecure feelings we often have of ourselves.

We've All Got Our Stuff — Some Of Us Just Hide It Better Than Others

The standards we hold of ourselves are derived from media images that don't exist in reality. How many times are we fed a Hollywood fairytale about someone and it feels as if our lives are miserable in comparison? And then, later, the truth of that person's life is revealed to have been a series of emotional challenges, setbacks, insecurities, disappointments, heartaches, losses, joys, victories, and breakthroughs. Like all of us.

The media is selling personas. Don't be fooled. Personas aren't real.

We equate celebrity with perfection. Becoming famous — through whatever means necessary — means we're guaranteed the byproducts of fame: privileges, material abundance, adoration and happiness. In short, *nirvana*. But just because we "make it" or become famous or win a million dollars or star in *America's Next Top Fill-in-the-Blank* doesn't mean the "stuff" we have goes away.

> *"I think everyone should get rich and famous and do everything they ever dreamed of so they can see that it's not the answer."*
> — **Jim Carrey,** *actor*

One of the profound things about life is that it's a great social equalizer. At some point, everyone has to face his or her stuff. As artists, we often have clearer insight into areas of our lives that require intense self-examination because these are areas we focus on — exploring more deeply, more intensely — in our work.

But for many of us, the struggle isn't necessarily in identifying where we get stuck, but how to get *unstuck*.

"I think you're born a shaman. The shaman goes down into the darkness for the tribe, to bring light and growth to the harvest. The difficulty in our culture is that, unlike the Native American culture and many others, it's not recognized and there's nobody to train you. So you're unconsciously a shaman for a long time, which often means you go down into the darkness and you don't know how to come back up."
— Andre Gregory, *theatre director*

The way "back up" is to keep going. To not give up. To stop measuring yourself against fantasies. To open our hearts. To examine and re-examine the beliefs we hold. About ourselves. About the things we've been taught. And about how we choose to see the world. To face head-on the things we most want to avoid. To know that we're bigger than the set of circumstances we face or the abusive thoughts we hold about ourselves. To realize that the only way out of something is through, never around.

My brother once asked me what it means to "open one's heart." What does that look like? It doesn't *look* like anything. It *feels* like something. It *feels* better to be more kind and generous to *yourself* first. It *feels* better to stop attacking yourself and beating yourself up for the mistakes you make. It *feels* lighter to stop judging yourself and others for where they are on their path.

It *feels* more encouraging to face your challenges with strength and optimism and not cynicism and bitterness and fear. You *feel* your way into your heart opening. And as you do, you see how often you've allowed it to be squeezed shut, to be twisted into an impenetrable knot; you realize the journey involves undoing those knots.

Meryl Streep has acknowledged that often when she accepts a film role she calls her agent in a panic right before she's set to start working to see if she can get out of her contract as she fears she's been miscast. Matt Damon has said that he couldn't even watch his early work without feeling as if he was going to vomit. When we see the image of Matt Damon that's projected to us, we assume he doesn't feel any of the "stuff" we're feeling. He must be beyond that.

> *"My agents were continuing to send me out for pilots. I had no money, no health insurance, and I was going on all these auditions for things I didn't believe in but that I was desperate for because I needed the work. As a result, I was shaky and intense and nervous and laughing or smiling too much, and I was making people uncomfortable. It was awkward. So my then agent called me in and sat me down — and in some ways it was great that she did this, because it put me back into a take-charge-of-this-situation mode — but she said, 'Honey, you're a great actress and I believe in you, so I took it upon myself to ask these people what's going on because you should be working. They're saying that you're too intense, that you want it too much.' And then she asked me, 'Are you*

worried about your age?' And I was like, 'Come on guys, leave my age out of it,' and I just started sobbing uncontrollably, like I'd reached absolute rock bottom. So I went back to my tiny little apartment in Venice {California}, and my mom, who was staying with me at the time, was like, 'Do not believe these people, Naomi. They cannot define you; they don't know you. So what if you're desperate and strange in the room. Of course you are — you're human!'"
— Naomi Watts, *actress*

The artist's journey requires us to uncover more and more of ourselves. Or sometimes, it uncovers it for us.

"What you do as an actor is what we are all trying to do as people. And what the artist tries to do is to get back, is to stop all that terrible self-conscious clothing we put on ourselves . . . {and} leave the most valuable purity behind, that great courage, that great open stuff."
— Dustin Hoffman, *actor*

"Great open stuff" is a great open heart. I would say, though, that it's not something that we're trying to do. It's something we already innately possess. We don't have to do anything. We just have to be awake and call it forth. Simply, bravely, honestly, *live* it.

Homework, Week 12: Spend one entire day — that's 24 hours — in silence. Some of you chatterboxes could even try 48 hours if you're feeling ambitious. But at the *very least*, try half a day. The best way to shatter some of the illusions you have about yourself and confront some of your fears is to jump into the exercise fully committed and stay silent for a full day. Besides, the nervousness or anxiousness or anything else you might tell yourself or might feel, is again, the ego trying to distract you from exploring something *beyond* its known structure.

Choose a day where the chances of your being disturbed will be minimal. Don't do this exercise on your birthday. If you have a roommate or are married, first explain to your housemate about what you're attempting and if you *must* communicate to someone, have paper and pen handy and write down your communication. But try to keep all dialogue (on paper) to a minimum.

If you think you're doing the exercise and you're actually walking around writing notes to everyone from the bank teller to the grocer as if you had laryngitis, then you aren't really exploring what it is to be in silence. If you think going to the movies by yourself and not talking for two hours is part of the homework, that's not quite right. Tuning in to mindless TV shows isn't it, either.

Try to keep *all* communication for one day to the absolute minimum. Be with yourself. Seek solitude. Don't seek the accompaniment of others. Or seek outer entertainment that so often is merely a distraction. See what it feels like to be in silence; how much energy and time you spend on mindless chatter or gossip or speak to relieve boredom. Become aware that as you get quiet, your thoughts will *seem* to get louder. You'll perhaps be harder on yourself or say more unkind things or feel as if you're going crazy.

But if you can stay with it, you'll begin to see that most of our errant, unfocused thoughts are pure distractions, grounded in nothing truthful or helpful. You'll begin to see them for what they truly are: a habituated machine that runs on autopilot without you ever stepping in to grab the reins and really examine what's going on up there.

Again, just observe and become aware of how the absence of language makes you feel. You might be surprised what you discover.

"You're just left with yourself all the time whatever you do anyway. You've got to get down to your own God in your own temple. It's all down to you mate."

— John Lennon

THE POSSIBLE DREAM

*"God can dream a bigger dream for you. Far
beyond anything you could ever imagine."*
— Oprah Winfrey

What is life, really, but one gigantic possibility? But we don't think about it in that way very often. We get so bogged down with the day-to-day world of surviving that we often view the world as mundane — thinking that nothing new or exceptional ever happens. But ask a scientist and he'll tell you differently.

*"There are only two ways to live your life. One
is as though nothing is a miracle. The other is
as though everything is a miracle."*
— **Albert Einstein**

Einstein will also tell you that quantum physics is the science or study of infinite possibilities from which reality and matter are born. From a scientific standpoint, then, the world in which we live is the quantum world of possibility.

Throughout this book I discuss how our outer reality is made up of the inner architecture of our minds. That is, what we think, we become. Artists and mystics have always known that there are levels of reality beyond what we see. And that everything we do see is born out of, or originates from, this space. Today, some scientists are using the word *consciousness* (something else I've talked about) to describe the birthing of phenomena in the material world. It's really a step *beyond* thinking. And they go on to discuss how objects in space and time (our world) are really waves of possibility.

"What converts possibility into actuality? When you see a chair, you see an actual chair, you don't see a possible chair. It is a paradox because who are we to do this conversion? We are nothing but the brain, which is made up of atoms and elementary particles. ...So how can a brain — which is made up of atoms and elementary particles — convert a possibility wave that it itself is? It itself is made up of the possibility waves of atoms and elementary particles, so it cannot convert its own possibility wave into actuality. Now in the new scientific view, consciousness is the ground of being. So who converts possibility into actuality? Consciousness does, because consciousness does not obey quantum physics. Consciousness is not made of material. Consciousness is transcendent. The material world of quantum physics is just possibility. It is consciousness, through the conversion of possibility into actuality, that creates what we see manifest. In other words, consciousness creates the manifest world."
— **Dr. Amit Goswami,** *physicist*

This scientific shift in seeing objects as waves of potential (as opposed to simply being seen as material objects) is becoming more commonplace.

"You're not an object — you are your consciousness. You're a unified being, not just your wriggling arm or foot, but part of a larger equation that includes all the colors, sensations, and objects you perceive. If you divorce one side of the equation from the other you cease to exist. Indeed, experiments confirm that particles only exist with real properties if they're observed. Until the mind sets the scaffolding of things in place, they can't be thought of as having any real existence — neither duration nor position in space. ...No phenomenon is a real phenomenon until it is an observed phenomenon. That's why in real experiments, not just the properties of matter — but space and time themselves — depend on the observer. Your consciousness isn't just part of the equation – the equation is you."
— **Robert Lanza,** *physicist*

People like to say that space is our last frontier. That's ridiculous. Man's own inner space — his mind — is the last frontier (and when I refer to the mind here, I'm not referring to the linear, calculating, rational, thinking aspect of our brain). Our *consciousness* is the last frontier. It's that space that goes beyond mind. It goes beyond reason.

So what's possible for us?

Everything. We don't have to be a physicist to understand that in the world of possibility, our thoughts (for the sake of simplicity, I'll continue to use thoughts as opposed to consciousness) determine our potential. They create our outer world of matter and experience. They are the building blocks of our world.

The Art Of Possibility

The art of possibility, really, is a science of restructuring thoughts that keep us tethered to scarcity thinking, and thus shutting out what's possible — into examining a situation from which we come away feeling empowered (and we've actually been learning the tools to do that throughout this book). It's about shifting from limiting paradigms (limiting systems of thought) to those that support our potential, which is infinite.

A paradigm shift doesn't mean being positive. It's not ignoring your negative thoughts. In the chapter on transformation, I discussed that authentic transformation occurs by working with your present (and often unwanted) condition. We aren't denying what is. A paradigm shift works in the same way, acknowledging a greater truth of who we really are in spite of (or really, because of) our incorrect thinking. This is very important to understand. We aren't denying that part of ourselves who believes, "No one wants me." The shift occurs in seeing that statement as one part of the paradigm. That is, embracing the untruth to discover the truth.

For example, merely changing "No one wants me," to "What do I have to contribute?" is not just about making a positive, warm, fuzzy statement. It's not about putting on a happy face and denying the negative energy behind that mask. It's an exercise in choosing differently. And a choice *is* possibility. The hundreds of choices we make daily create unseen possibilities and out of those lived possibilities come still more choices and still more possibilities.

Why Can't I Ever Get Away From Me?

The truth is, we can never get to where we'd like to be except by starting in the place we're currently residing — emotionally, psychologically and spiritually. There's no escaping your Self. We can move to another city or get another girlfriend or change jobs, but the common denominator in all these experiences is the Self. The Self comes with us and all the things we think, feel, and believe about ourselves, whether based in truth or not.

The areas we want to avoid in life — the "bad" stuff — the "negativity"— are really the grist that creates a transformation to move into a "positive" experience. We're unfortunately programmed to avoid pain and hurt at all costs. We constantly seek out pleasure (even if it's ultimately a destructive pleasure, like drug abuse) instead of acknowledging that pain is a part of life's process. It shouldn't be avoided but accepted, in order to help us get on with what we need to get on with.

Since we know that all suffering is caused by attachments and that all attachments are in time (this relative world) and that time eventually ends (we don't stay here forever, folks), then there's going to be pain. Like it or not, this is the matrix of the world in which we're living. It's a part of our human experience here — all of it — so why try to avoid it? And why would we want to? The sorrows in life have as equally a profound effect on us as our joys. And as discussed, joy can't be fully understood without having experienced sadness. So it's all essential. Our only alternative would be *not* to live if we didn't accept pain as a part of this existence.

"Myths tell us how to confront and bear and interpret suffering, but they do not say that in life there can or should be no suffering. You're not going to get rid of it. Who — when or where — has ever been quit of the suffering of life in this world?"
— Joseph Campbell

When it comes to possibility, then, it's important to recognize our own power of choice. Both the "negative" and "positive" polarities of life experiences help us to choose. But often when we want to choose something more uplifting, something more hopeful, the ego rears its ugly head and forces us to choose something more fearful, more depressing. I've discussed the ego throughout this book but I think it's important to touch on it again.

Simply, the ego doesn't want us to believe that something is possible.

Leggo My Ego

Ego comes from the Greek word meaning "small and separate." A small and separate self. Haven't we all felt small when we lash out at someone or are petty? Haven't we all felt separate and alone when we feel as if we suffer the weight of the world on our shoulders (poor me) or when no one understands us? Or when we're stubbornly convinced that we're "right" and that other person's "wrong?" The ego is skilled in keeping us small and separate by our identification with it and its "problems." It distracts us from the present moment — which is full of possibility — and makes us hypercritical of our actions.

> *"While you are acting, you don't second-guess yourself; you don't waste your time wondering whether you made the right decision. You're done deciding — now you're acting: Be present with your actions. After you've finished, if you want to, you can sit back and reflect and say, 'Was that the right choice?' That's different. But while you're doing it, do it fully. When you're making tea, make tea. When you're brushing your teeth, brush your teeth. When you're making love, make love. Big acts, small acts, whatever it is, be fully there with it. Stop ruining things for yourself with the self-conscious, judgmental holding back. What we're letting go of in that process is the old, self-critical inner voice, the old superego that's so afraid of blowing it, afraid of making a mistake, afraid of looking like a fool. The judging superego is incompatible with acting in the moment."*
> — **Ram Dass,** *spiritual teacher*

He might as well have been talking to actors, but is actually referring to all people about becoming conscious with what they're doing.

All of the ego's makeup — its function — is fear-based protection. Even at the expense of our own happiness. Any thoughts that might threaten the ego's presumption it's running the show — when it isn't — is potentially dangerous. This is because literally, its livelihood's at stake.

We've misidentified with the ego as being *who I am* and it'll do whatever it has to do to keep us believing that lie.

Stop Re-Writing (And Re-Interpreting) History

Ego likes to write fiction. After an intense emotional scene in class in which an actor hasn't allowed him or herself to be affected, I've heard such excuses as, "I can't feel," or "That's not possible for me," or "I'm not able to cry." The ego tells us something isn't possible for us emotionally to move into. Of course the ego's going to say that. It's too scary.

It sucks sometimes to receive criticism, but there it is. Often our first reaction — the ego reaction — is to defend ourselves from someone's perceived attack. Why? Because we've become invested in the external things that we think define us. When those externals are questioned, the ego is threatened, associating the questioning with danger. It views it as an implicit assault on what it's spent a great deal of time and energy building.

An observation or a critique becomes a personal attack. Ouch. The truth is, critiques enable us to grow and realize what's possible. But for the ego, they trigger associative memories that have nothing to do with what's actually being said to us in that present moment. We're brought back to a moment in our life (generally childhood) when we were shamed for behaving a certain way or doing something others labeled "bad" or expressing ourselves in a manner that wasn't deemed "appropriate." Often we were punished for it. That emotional memory is triggered and we misconstrue a talk *now* for a talk we had with our parents when we were 12 and felt (or were made to feel) ashamed, embarrassed, unloved or unsafe.

Enough About Me . . . What Do You Think About Me?

The ego's job is to make it all about the individual and his needs, his desires, his views, his goals, his opinions, his worries. I may sound like I'm doing a little bit of ego-bashing here, but understand that as long as we live in this body there will be an ego. It serves a purpose in our developmental maturation. But what I'm talking about is being able to make the distinction between the ego self (me, me, me, me and more me) and something greater than the ego.

Some people are so egocentric that they aren't even aware that there's another part of themselves waiting to be experienced. When I say egocentric it means focused, or centered on, or overly identified with, the ego. When we operate purely from ego consciousness — or *lack* of consciousness, that is — it's as if we're moving through life in darkness. There's a veil that separates us from the light. The ego is the veil wanting to remain drawn closed in order to obscure us from our light.

"What about me?" is a line we find ourselves saying often in life and it's pure ego. What if we tried, "How can I help?" It's very difficult to be living from a place of possibility when it's filtered from "What do I get out of it?" It's self-centered, which is centering on the ego, which isn't the higher Self.

Here's a diagram that helps us understand ego and why it works best (does it ever work best?) when we have the awareness that it's a *part* of our Self, but not our entire being.

This diagram shows how to realign with possibility. In the drawing on the left — the "Big E"— mistakenly identifies our selves as the big EGO with perhaps a tiny awareness of our authentic self. In this model, the focus, the energy, the magnetic force, if you will, is all pointing inwards to the big E.

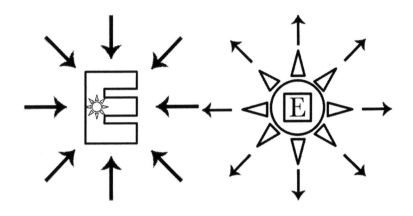

The authentic Self that resides within the E is radiating outward but it's overshadowed by the bigger pull of the arrows that are all pointing at the E — the Ego. *Look at Me!* This is how we spend a great deal of our time. In extreme cases people are so ego-identified they're clinically self-obsessed or narcissistic. Their ego completely overwhelms the part of them that is loving, non-judgmental, fearless, giving. The part that seeks solutions rather than problems derived from a separate self.

Have you ever noticed that our ego simultaneously makes us feel pumped up (artificially as it all comes from external sources) while at the same time (if we're aware) it attacks us with bouts of low self-esteem and self-hate. Talk about a bizarre mind game.

The diagram on the right, however, represents who we actually all are, even when we forget and the ego takes over and turns us into indignant, self-important monsters. The drawing on the right radiates outward. One's energy, one's flow, reaches outward to help others. It's expansive. It's a model of contributing, of giving, of sharing ourselves. We're not withholding. And when we're tapped into this state of awareness we feel empowered, ecstatic, courageous, beautiful, talented, and intelligent.

Don't You Know Who I Think I Am?

Artists are here to contribute. When we do, we're empowered. The casting director has a casting problem, that's why she's seeing actors in the first place. When we enter a room and really try to contribute by helping them solve their problem, our presence changes. In other words, we become the solution to their problem when we're creating from a place of pure moment-to-moment expression. But if our ego leads the way, "Will they like me?" or "What will they think of me?" or "How do I look?" or "Am I saying this the wrong way?" or "Do I look stupid?" the ego's self-protection wins out and we end up shutting out possibility.

Possibility is service because you have something unique to share. It's then still *all about you* — but from an authentic place that transcends ego. Suddenly, all your preoccupations with how you look fall away. That's one of the ego's main purposes: to keep us looking good. But once you realize the casting office (or music producer or gallery owner) actually wants *you* — that's why they called *you* in — you're liberated from the worry of what others think. You simply stop caring. The ego doesn't get in the way of you authentically creating. Your energy begins radiating outwards. It's like dropping a rock into a lake and the waves ripple outward from the source. It continues to ripple out into a larger area, affecting more and more people (and it comes back to us – fulfilling this principle that the energy we put out is the energy we receive). Isn't that a fantastic image of the power we authentically possess in positively affecting the lives of others?

(As a side note, no one's really thinking about us nearly as much as our ego would like us to believe anyway. In a given 24-hour period, who do you think about the most? Final Answer: *yourself!* So who do you think people are most thinking about? Hate to break it to you: *themselves!*)

The Seven-Headed Ego Dragon

Sometimes people mistakenly think ego only takes the form of the pompous, obnoxious, arrogant, loud personality that we've all known (or been). But in reality, ego has many faces. Which one runs our life? We play the role of the victim: "Oh, I can't do this." Or the martyr: "Don't worry about me, I'll be fine." Sometimes it's the unworthy one: "She'll never go out with someone like me." Or the defiant one: "I'm never going to open my heart to anyone ever again." Any patterns that keep us from experiencing the greater part of who we are can be traced to the workings of the ego.

"The ego is the power of our own minds turned against us, pretending to be our champion, yet in reality undermining all of our hopes and dreams. ...It is in reality the embodiment of our self-hatred. The ego sees itself as different and special, always justified at keeping the world at bay. Seeing ourselves as separate, we subconsciously attract and interpret circumstances that seem to bear out that belief."
— **Marianne Williamson**, *author*

By now this distinction should be clearer: we just keep getting more of what we believe. But because we aren't taught how to identify that other part of ourselves that is *not* the ego, it can be like meeting a long-lost cousin when we discover that there is another part of who we are. Something *beyond* the ego.

Power Plays

Nowadays, everything is "power this" and "power that:" "power yoga," "power shakes," "power Pilates," "power lunches." Patanjali, the founder of yoga more than 2,000 years ago, would probably contort himself into a yogic pretzel-twist if he could hear how the misuse of this word "power" was being used in conjunction with yoga — which literally means the *union with Self.*

We mistakenly think that power in our culture is attained by achievement. But power is an illusion bound by the ego. It exists and can only be maintained through our external identification with things. That is, our power is "pumped in" to us from the trappings of the external world we strive to control and dominate. So power, in my explanation, is like an aggressive force or action that we perpetrate. "I am powerful, so I can get the perfect table at this month's most 'in' restaurant, or be able to buy an entire office building, or get the president of a multi-million dollar corporation to call me back immediately." Our association with who we are and what we can do (to others) is based on externals. Take the titles, the tables, and the phone calls away and someone then starts to feel powerless if his only identification is with the things outside himself.

Empowerment, on the other hand, is the authentic strength derived from an internal source. It can't be taken away. It's independent of external factors. It's really a state of being, a state of awareness that leaves us feeling alive and awake to the present — not from being the boss, or firing people, but from something inside that emanates outwardly. "Power" often involves dominion over other people or things. An empowered person, on the other hand, shares him-*Self* and empowers other people to do the same. He knows he doesn't "own" anything.

Oprah Winfrey is a great example of the difference between these two words. To most, because of her money, influence, possessions, and properties, she's viewed as "powerful." At an external, material level, she is. I mean she practically owns the world. But because she inspires people to discover who they are and transform their lives, to share their spirit, and pursue their dreams, she's "empowered" *and* empowering.

When we meet authentically empowered people we often don't know how to respond, because many of us haven't been given the tools to uncover our own sense of empowerment. These people may scare or intimidate us. We may find that we're full of judgments about them because they intrinsically bring up our own sense of unfulfilled potential. We become agitated or frustrated or jealous or depressed. We know instinctually that we're capable of such greatness but our ego would rather have us feeling threatened than awaken our inner slumbering giant.

I love the Polynesian proverb: "You are sitting on a whale fishing for minnows." That's such a great example of the power of the ego. It keeps us missing our opportunity for possibility. We can't see that we're sitting on a whale. Actually, we *are* the whale. Our potential is whale-like: enormous. Yet, we're so distracted by the little stuff (our worries, our grievances, our judgments) that we're unaware of the giant who resides within each of us.

What would happen if we simply started looking for bigger fish?

Homework, Week 13: Today and every day for the next week, be in service. What does that mean? Simply give without any desire to get paid back in any way. The world will give you ample opportunities.

You don't have to go to the soup kitchen and feed the homeless, unless you want to. Just go about living your day and you'll see how the universe will supply you with an abundance of experiences in which you can contribute. Perhaps in the past you would have ignored them or pretended they didn't exist. Or maybe you weren't even aware you were being called to service. Maybe you've walked past a homeless man. He asked you for money and you ignored him. Today, give him some money. Or buy him some food. You're sitting in traffic and someone is trying to squeeze in front of you. Allow them to cut ahead this time. You're at the grocery store and the person behind you only has four items in her cart. Let her go before you. Tell the person who makes your latte every day, "I really appreciate the work you do." Buy someone flowers just because. Put money in someone else's meter without them knowing. Tell a stranger on the bus she has a pretty smile. Or looks nice.

You don't have to think about things to come up with. As you engage in the world, opportunities for you to express yourself selflessly will present themselves. Just be awake to them and say "yes." You may, for the first time, feel a swelling in your heart that comes simply from the exhilaration of giving. It's our natural state. Sadly, we are so oriented toward "What can I get out of this?" that we miss the connections with other people that want to take us to that feeling place within ourselves. Observe that the act of serving really connects you to you. Do this at least seven times this week. Or more.

You may discover a new lease on life. Sharing with others is truly an indescribable joy. And while you're sharing, you'll begin to see that you truly *do* make a difference.

"Make voyages! Attempt them!
There's nothing else."
— Tennessee Williams

HOW DO I GET OUT OF MY OWN WAY? LET ME COUNT THE WAYS

"Creativity requires the courage to let go of certainties."
— Erich Fromm

Why do we make such a big deal about tiny disturbances in our life? They amount to nothing more than a minor speed bump in the totality of our lives (getting upset about a parking ticket, a cancelled flight, an unexpected fender bender, spilled coffee, a long line at the bank) — and yet we make them *the thing* in our lives? Why are we programmed to focus on what isn't working when so much is? When our stuff gets triggered in life — which is invariable (and essential) — it's helping us on our journey. But how we choose to work through our challenges can be made easier. And less stressful. More enlightening. More fun. "Fun? When the shit hits the fan, it doesn't feel fun, Tony." But there is a way out and the discovery of that process can be liberating and, yes, fun.

I hope you haven't been a slacker and the homework is helping, so that when you're in the middle of a meltdown, you stay on the upside and not let it pull you into a darkened abyss. Or maybe it still pulls you into the abyss but rather than staying there for days — which maybe was your previous tendency (sleeping for 18 hours and binging on brownies and lighting the bong) — you now only get stuck for an hour or two. And you're bong-free. That's progress.

If the homework hasn't been enough, let's examine 25 *more* ways to assist you in getting out of your own way in life. If you could just commit to any of these exercises over a period of 30 days, you would see a major shift in how you deal with stress, mood swings, and negativity. You'd have access to facing your challenges in life in a less upsetting and more peaceful and balanced way. You'd create new brain circuitry, which in turn, would give us access to more good-feeling emotion.

Attunement. It means *to bring into harmony*. To tune the instrument. What are we but simply instruments, waiting to be tuned? Life experiences are gifts to use in attuning our hearts and minds, our emotional, and spiritual selves to a deeper part within. Upsetting events — to the ego — are unwanted. To our higher Self, they are needed (and actually *wanted*). They tune us. The goal is not to let the fine-tuning break our string. A lot of that process is by choosing a thought that makes us feel better about the explanation of the unwanted events occurring in our lives. And as we know, the ego's job is to keep us out of tune by rationalizing and defending positions that keep us stuck and unhappy.

So it's about choosing happiness. Sometimes we don't have access to those better-feeling thoughts because we are so in our stuff. So let's look at how else we can use our stuff to help us move beyond it.

1)   **Meditation.** Revisit week two homework. Nothing is more important than going within. *Nothing.*

2)   **Take a walk.** I mentioned earlier that when Einstein was stuck on a problem he couldn't solve, he'd push his chair from the table, put down his pen, stand up and go take a walk. When he came back to tackle the problem some time later, the answer he was looking for was suddenly there. Why? Partly because our left brain becomes so engrossed in tackling a problem that it blocks any sort of access to higher understanding, which is namely, the right brain. The right

hemisphere is connected to the universal matrix of which we are all a part. It wants to provide the answers you seek, but the impenetrability of the left brain discounts that world. Indeed, the left brain doesn't even want to acknowledge that another world exists.

But what happens when you free up the energy that's been attacking a problem for so long? The energy begins to move and drop into different parts of your body, recalibrating itself and shifting to equalize and restore balance. By taking a walk, your somatic nervous system takes over, fires neurons with commands and lessens the stranglehold of the left brain. It relinquishes its power, which allows you to access information from the right brain that isn't available when the left brain is in hyper-overdrive.

Try it. The next time you are pissed off at your boss or in a rage about your ex, take a walk. The next time you feel bored or uninspired, take a walk. You'll be surprised to find that portals to a new world open up in the form of signs, ideas, hunches, intuition, and even practical information. The question is, will you listen?

3) **Breathe.** Sounds simple but how often do we take for granted the function that is keeping us alive? We're rarely mindful of our breathing, which is maybe not a bad thing as it does it on its own. But when we're stressed or feeling overwhelmed, we get in the way of the breathing apparatus performing its function. We breathe from the shoulders up. We don't inhale deeply.

So the next time you begin to feel yourself go into your head and out of your body because of some trigger, simply focus first on your breathing. Become aware of how you are not using the diaphragm properly. As you inhale deeply the diaphragm moves downward, pulling the ribs up and outward. Feel your lungs fill with air. Inhale slowly, counting to 10. Exhale, counting to 10. Do this 10 times. Your shoulders shouldn't move. As you do, it again diffuses the energy from the left brain and drops your energy into your body. You begin to feel more relaxed and calm. Observe how something that seemed like a "problem" is now not nearly so dramatic.

4) **Reinterpret the thought.** Find a new way of interpreting a situation that you are convinced is your fault or makes you feel as if you are unlovable, or untalented or a loser. Years ago, I went out on a few dates with this guy who was funny and nice and I thought — at the time — a keeper. I never heard from him again. I immediately took the brain drain train, "What's wrong with me?" "I'm unattractive." "No one's ever going to love me." I expended a lot of energy beating myself up and making myself feel inadequate and further confirming my worst fears (and lies) about myself. Eventually, I got over it.

Fast forward to three years later. I run into this same guy. Out of the blue he says, "Hey Tony. I'm sorry about what happened a few years ago. I was really going through some rough stuff and I didn't even know how to show up in my own life. I'm sober now and just wanted to make amends." How awesome is that? Not that he suffered and had a few rough years, but that he overcame it and made amends. His honesty helped reveal truth to me. I wasn't awful. I wasn't a freak. It wasn't my fault.

The moral of the story, though, is next time, try to interpret events correctly when they first happen so you don't end up beating yourself up for untruths you tell yourself. We never have the full story, folks. It's more truthful — and accurate — to tell a story that affirms us, rather than telling one that tears us apart. And the truth is, it never has anything to do with us anyway.

5) **Fake it 'til you make it.** I often use this analogy in acting class. If you can't get to a feeling that you are required to get to, then fake it. The *commitment* to faking something will get you to the real thing. Always. Science proves that if your body and face take on the properties of a certain feeling then your body will begin to produce that feeling chemically. So if I start to scrunch my face into a pout and then force it harder into a grimace or expression of anguish, my body will react by sending out endorphins that match the feeling aspect of my face. So I might genuinely start to feel sad and upset and heart-broken. So it is in life. Sometimes, we have to really fake ourselves into feeling better. If you commit to moving the energy in your body into something else, your body will take on a new feeling. An example is singing. I rarely hear people singing sad songs in the shower. (If you lean toward singing co-dependent power love ballads that make you want to slit your wrists then *change the record*.) As we sing, we connect to a more joyful, expansive, celebratory part of our nature. Even if you suck at it. Sing. Sing until you start to feel better.

It's important to remember: you don't get what you wish for in life; you get what you believe. Sometimes, it takes a while (and a bit of practice) to change our beliefs and allow them to grow into something wonderful. Start with smaller beliefs. As you feel more confident, your beliefs will naturally expand to start encompassing larger possibilities. Even if you don't have the material evidence in life to yet show you that something is possible for you, just fake it. When we were kids we used to pretend all the time. Try it again as an adult. Pretend. Behind every little pretend is a little bit of truth.

6) **Connect to your body.** An actress in class recently had an emotional breakthrough in her work where she really allowed herself to feel and express deep emotion. Afterwards, she said she was having an "out-of-body-experience". *Wrong.*

She actually had an "*in*-her-body-experience" by allowing herself to feel. When we spend so much time in our heads, we disengage from our body and our emotional self. The more we connect with our body, the less in our heads we will be. (And again, science has shown that physical exercise releases "good feeling" endorphins.) So do anything that gets you connected to the physical. Dance. Go for a run. Go to the gym. Take yoga. Swim. Move your body. Get a massage. Your spirit will move with it and so will your feelings.

7) **Visualization.** When your reality bites the big one, spend more time visualizing what you would like your future to look like. The reality may be that right now you don't have a girlfriend or a lot of money or a good job or a creative outlet. Spend more time envisioning your world the way you would like it to be. If you do this for five minutes every day, it would radically change your external reality.

As you dream it, focus on the feelings that are engendered by having the things you want. Focus on what it feels like to marry your dream date or have a new car or get your own TV series. Flood your body with the exciting, joyful feelings that come with these expectations. Why do we spend time dreaming up doom-and-gloom scenarios? Doesn't it just naturally feel more fun to dream hopeful ones instead?

8) **Change the subject. Completely.** I once got into an argument with a friend and every time I heard her name my whole body would go into some sort of weird emotional seizure. The more I talked about her, the more I'd get upset, wanting to scream and throw things, and drive off a cliff — preferably with her in the passenger seat and me jumping ship right at the last moment. What I learned is that the more I stewed and talked about and re-visited the experience, the more upset I'd become. Sometimes hot-topic

buttons within get pushed *anytime* they are discussed. So until you can move through that phase of the disturbance, see if you can just change the subject.

The next time someone wants to talk to you about your friend who "did you wrong," see if you can just let it go completely and not discuss it. It's going to take some training, at first, because we like to get everyone within earshot to be on our side and join forces in lambasting that person and supporting us in sending her over the cliff. But with discipline and the understanding that the most important thing is that we choose to feel good, we will be able to forgive, let go, and actually find peace.

9) **Focus on what *is* working.** Take a moment to breathe into what's working in your life. You wear designer jeans and take trips to Manhattan and to the Jersey Shore and you even get to watch *Jersey Shore*. Don't be oriented toward what is lacking. If you celebrate what is working, you'll see those areas that seem to be lacking will start to transform into something else. If you can't find anything that's worth celebrating then go visit a developing country. Go to remote parts of the world. See that more than 80% of the world's population survives on less than $10 a day. Then tell me you have nothing to celebrate.

10) **Look for the power of synchronicity in your life (and write it down).** What makes events synchronous is that they are unlikely to occur together by chance. What makes them meaningful is that at some level they represent things you may desire in life or illustrate the nature of your relationship to these things. They are often communicated through signs and symbols urging you to follow the path they are revealing. It's your job to investigate what significance they have and what they personally mean to you. At a

superficial level, they demonstrate that we are co-creators at a causal level in our lives. They give meaning to the phrase, "the universe is always giving you what you want." When you have no attachment to it — and are therefore not blocking its manifestation — it shows up in your material world.

You may be thinking, "Well, that's swell, but how do I apply this to the things I really desire in life?" Stop creating so much energy around what isn't there. The more you doubt and question the thing you desire, the further it moves away from you. When you have a thought about someone or something and it creates a desire, and with the desire comes an attachment and a doubt, you are, in effect, cauterizing your intention for that thing to manifest. The doubt and simultaneous attachment to it is an implicit command to the universe that you really don't believe you can have this thing. It's as if you are canceling out that which you are ordering.

Watch, as you let go of control, how synchronicities will occur with greater and greater frequency. Follow them. Acknowledge them. Write them down. They're trying to show you a road map of your life. See where they lead you. Your life can become fun again. An adventure. You're a co-creator with the universe. If you're creating at this level, you can continue to create at higher and higher levels as well.

11) **Write.** Just write. It doesn't matter what you write. Simply write your feelings down. You don't have to worry if it makes sense or tells a story or is a screenplay. Just write down the things you feel and are thinking about in life. It's like walking. It frees up the mental mind game you play with yourself and gives you clarity. Put it on the page.

12) **Write down your goals.** In addition to writing whatever it is you want to write about, also write down goals. They

keep you focused and on task. If you can think them you can achieve them.

13) **Write down 100 things you are grateful for.** Gratitude for things we have in our lives is a sure way of allowing more things to flow to you.

14) **Live today as if it were your last.** If today were your last day on the planet, would you still choose to harbor resentments? Would you still be too scared to express yourself? Would you try to hide your authentic feelings? Would you be concerned with how other people perceive you? Would you be judgmental about your own self-expression? Would you be concerned with being a failure if you attempted to try something? Would you cross to the other side of the street if you saw someone you didn't want to see? We're like squirrels gathering our nuts for some future winter. Well, what if that future never came? You'd have a lot of stored nuts you never gave away. You'd never have shared what is unique and special about you. Stop being so self-oriented. Stop holding your nuts. Give them away.

15) **Live it "as if."** At one level it is. In other words, if you desire something, the mere fact that you can desire it means it already exists in the material universe somewhere. If it didn't, you wouldn't be able to desire it. The fact that you thought of it proves it exists. No one is thinking an original thought. At one level, it's all been thought before, because thought is causal. The work is aligning with what you desire. And you align by feeling what it feels like to already have that thing in your life. So live it as if you already have it.

16) **Fight for your happiness.** Sometimes you have to fight like a honey badger to be happy. It's so much easier to fall

into our default habits — our negative feedback loop — by being a whiner or complainer or a victim. Snap out of it. Fight when you fall into one of those days. Fight when it'd be so much easier to just get stuck in our neural groove. All it takes is a little bit of will power.

17) **Keep stepping to the right of your left hemisphere.**

"By stepping to the right of our left brains, we can all uncover the feelings of well- being and peace that are so often sidelined by our own brain chatter."
— **Jill Bolte Taylor,** *brain scientist*

As a neuroanatomist who studies the brain, she should know. And as further evidence, she suffered a stroke and experienced first-hand what it is to travel back and forth between both hemispheres of the brain. When you step to the right of your left hemisphere, you are plugged into something bigger than your ego-identification needs. Bigger than your little self. You are a part of the intuitive, creative, omniscient world of infinite possibility. But in order to access that world, you have to quiet the noise the left brain creates, preventing us from hearing what it is we need to hear. Right brain is what you want. Start making more right brain choices.

18) **Talk about your vision splendid.** A vision splendid is simply the visualization that you have for yourself. The most amazing life that you can dream for yourself is indeed a splendid vision. Isn't it more fun to talk about what's possible than bitching about what isn't working? Doesn't it make you feel more hopeful and excited to celebrate the

things that can come to you as opposed to focusing on what isn't yet here? Isn't it more invigorating to talk about what your life can be than to constantly complain about what you don't have? So call up a friend and talk about your life as if it's the most splendid thing ever. Because, truthfully, it is.

19) **Don't give energy to things that aren't working.** The interesting thing about life is that very often when you just let go of things that are troubling you, they will work themselves out naturally on their own. If they don't, they will eventually come back to you in a different way or different form and at another time. And if you are continuing to evolve, when they do come back, you will then have the tools to deal with them in a more effectual way. So just practice more letting go.

20) **Have friends who will call you on your stuff.** I don't mean friends who will point out things about you they don't like (although that can be helpful too). I'm talking about friends who will engage in a dialogue with you and point you in the direction towards what *is* working in your life when you get stressed or caught up in your drama and can't see a way out. The people who support you in your victimization, defense, rationalizations, excuses or ego-based fears aren't really your friends. You want to cultivate relationships that challenge you to keep climbing to higher levels of your being.

My good friend, Suzanne, was very upset and stressed out about having a baby. She and her husband had been trying (to no avail) to get pregnant for over a year. One day she was completely consumed by the idea that she would never get pregnant. I believe that she secretly wanted me to corroborate her point of view and support her in her (unfounded) misery. I refused. Mostly because it was easy for me to maintain a vision for her that I knew was possible. From where I stood, it seemed like a no-brainer. If she eventually could just let go and relax about the whole situation, she would get pregnant. (I know this was easy for me to say because I wasn't in her situation feeling her grief and fear.) But that's the point. As her friend, I chose not to go into that delusion with her and instead kept holding the possibility that she would get pregnant. A month or two later, she did. I hated to say,

"Suzanne . . . I told you so," but I did. And it felt good. Get your friends to support you in your vision. Not in what's not working.

21) **Be in service.** Start helping others with no agenda. Start giving in life what you want to receive. You want more love? Then start giving more love. You want more support? Then start supporting others. Watch how the act of service transforms your life.

22) **Commit.** It's much easier to *act* your way into a new way of thinking than to *think* your way into a new way of acting. The more you sit around and think about things, the less likely you are to act on them. Get into the world of action. Don't worry about the end results. Don't worry that the thing you want isn't going to show up. The more you take action, the more something will come out of the action.

"Failure is an option, but fear is not."
— James Cameron, *filmmaker*

Failure is the other side of success. You can't have success without failure. It's not this separate experience that we're trying to avoid in life. Without failures we wouldn't be able to have victories. And a deeper truth lies in the axiom that within each failure is the seed to our future success.

Long before James Cameron made the biggest movie ever (*Avatar*), he made a real stinker called *Piranha 2.* Does anyone remember that movie? Does anyone care? The point is, had he let fear stop him, he would have never created (and we never would have seen) *Avatar.*

23) **Let no one in (or out) of "the business" define you.** Life's too short to stay in relationship with people who don't support you. Who don't celebrate your success. Who lack a spirit of generosity and authentic joy for the artistic victories you achieve in life. Sometimes this may be a lover. Or a friend. Or a family member. It sucks when you discover people who are close to you often seem to undermine your accomplishments. It can be painful.

It goes without saying that there are enough people out there who won't support you on your journey. If there are people in your personal life who fit that description, try telling them how you feel. If they can't alter their behavior (or at least *fake it*), try taking a break from them. Surround yourself with affirmative people who see what's possible for you. If you meet — or work with (and you will) — a horrible boss or a duplicitous friend, a bad manager, producer, or acting teacher for that matter, don't walk — run! — in the other direction. Never look back. Even if that person happens to be someone you perceive as "powerful."

Remember your self-worth. Value who you are as a human being first. An actor second. A musician second. A designer second. A painter second. Don't ever subject yourself to anyone or any comment that marginalizes you, diminishes you, makes you doubt yourself, or tries to break your spirit. You're not just a commodity. Humanity comes in all shapes and sizes and colors and ages. Remember that.

24) **Keep your heart open.** Don't let the supposed "decision makers" make you feel bad about yourself because you don't fit the descriptions they say they're looking for. The best advice I can give is to just keep your heart open. When your boyfriend pisses all over your dreams, keep your heart open. When you've been rejected for a job for the most superficial of reasons, keep your heart open. When someone you feel who has less talent than you gets the job you auditioned for, keep it open. When the younger, hotter, more networking-savvy actress gets the agent and you still don't have one, keep it open.

Don't worry that keeping your heart open might mean you'll be perceived as a bleeding heart. Or push-over. Or a Pollyanna. Worry instead when these same experiences start closing your heart. Or they start making you cynical. Or skeptical. Or pessimistic. Or jealous. Or jaded. Or hyper-critical. Or angry. Or bitter. Or a complainer. Worry about your heart being lost in this quagmire of self-pity, never to be opened again.

"Your work is to discover your work and then with all your heart to give yourself to it."
— **The Buddha**

You can't do that with a closed heart.

25) **Have as much fun as you can. Always. And all ways.** Life is meant to be fun. And so is creating. It's the reason we were interested in performing (or painting or writing or singing) in the first place. This truth — this *spirit* of joy — is the most important aspect to keep in our hearts. We can let so many other factors rob us of our joy: critics saying cruel

things about our physical attributes, teachers who belittle us, directors who bully us, or simply the constant arbitrary rejections that face any artist in any field. These external factors — compounded and multiplied — can distract us from the original intent to create. But they can also build character and uncover inner resources we never knew we possessed.

So don't take them on as your truth but regard them instead as mere stepping-stones. All artists are special in that our spirited will to create in a monetary world based on business and not art, *is* remarkable. What we can express *is* remarkable. Just have fun with it. You can't fail. You can't lose. An artist expressing his truth can never fail. Just have fun playing and expressing who you are. I couldn't think of a more noble calling and a more worthy challenge. And really, that's what life's meant to be.

Homework, Week 14: You have 25 different techniques to assist you in getting out of your own way and living a more joyous, passionate, energetic life this week. Don't take my word for it. Try any of them when you are feeling stuck or sluggish or depressed or you're throwing yourself a gigantic pity party because of some perceived slight in your life. Get activated by applying one of these ways to reframe the events that occur in your life and refocus so that you begin to overcome your challenges and not feel defeated by them.

When I began to meditate I went through a two-week period of fantasy and hopeful delusion. I assumed that since I was learning to sit in silence, my life would become stress-free. I would no longer face any more challenges. My life would be a breeze because I was becoming a little Yogi.

Imagine my shock when shit still happened. I still had to deal with my problems, my challenges. I still had goals to reach and obstacles to overcome. They didn't disappear just because I was meditating every day.

But what I *did* discover is that my *attitude* in dealing with my challenges began to change. I started to have more patience. I saw that things didn't upset me like they used to. I felt a greater sense of peace pervade me while tackling problems. I found myself being less reactive and *dramatic*.

So apply some of these distinctions this week as you experience your life. See if you can begin replacing some of your habituated, reactive, often negative responses to life's events with greater ease because of these 25 concepts.

The problems may not necessarily change. But *you* will.

"The essence of all beautiful art, all great art, is gratitude."
— Friedrich Nietzsche

PARTLY SUNNY SKIES

"Gamble everything for love if you're a true human being."
— Rumi

As we come to a close, it might be helpful to remember a few points we've covered on this journey. We've identified ways to connect to who we are by different means. We've talked about peak experiences, living moment-to-moment, silence, letting go of the ego, listening, surrendering, intuition, and many other distinctions that connect us to the greater part of who we are. Hopefully, we are now at least intellectually aware (if not more conscious) of the fact that who we are has nothing to do with our external trappings.

I'm not my job, my title, the amount of money I earn, what kind of car I drive, my age, my gender, my moods, my likes and dislikes, my problems, and so on. Even though they're terms we associate with ourselves, the shift in our life comes when we tap into the space within that transcends our identification with these externals and allow ourselves to be expressed beyond them.

The easiest way to realize our potential is by putting aside some time daily to sit in silence. It's in the silence that we can break our identification with the external definitions that block and sometimes imprison us.

"An old Hindu legend says there was a time when men were gods. But they abused their divine powers so much that Brahma, the master of all gods, decided to take these powers away and hide them in a place where they would be impossible to find. All that remained was to find a suitable hiding place. A number of lesser gods were appointed to a council to deal with the issue. They suggested this: 'Why not bury man's powers in the earth?' To which Brahma replied, 'No, that will not do because man would dig deep and find it.' So the gods said, 'In that case, we will send their divinity to the deepest depths of the ocean.' But Brahma replied again, 'Sooner or later man will explore the depths of the ocean and it is certain he will find it and bring it to the surface.' So the lesser gods concluded, 'Neither land nor sea is a place where man's divine powers will be safe, so we do not know where to hide it.' At that moment Brahma exclaimed, 'This is what we will do with man's divinity! We will hide it deep within him because that is the only place he will not think to look.' From then on, according to the legend, man searched the world over; he explored, climbed, dove, and dug in search of something that was inside himself all along."
— Eric Butterworth, *theologian*

All the great work any artist has ever achieved — from Michelangelo to Mozart — has come from his inner fount of creativity, his inner source of inspiration. So why wouldn't we want to go within? Mostly because the external stimuli that stirs our world has such a primal hold and can be so intoxicating that we don't realize there's another world, far more fulfilling, awaiting our attention. By maintaining a practice where we go inward every day, we can tap into and release this storehouse of artistic potential.

A New Mind

A friend recently told me she can't quiet her mind no matter how hard she tries. It may seem a daunting task at first, because the outer world has such a pull on us. "She's hot." "He's sexy!" "That cake looks delicious." "That coffee smells good." "I want to buy those jeans I saw in the Old Navy commercial." And on and on it goes.

My friend thinks sitting in silence isn't productive; that she's wasting time. This is another example of the mind wanting to be in charge. If we engage in a practice that's trying to quiet the mental noise, the mind's first reaction is to get louder to combat its perceived threat. My friend's paradox — like for many of us — is that until she quiets her mind, it's almost impossible to become more attuned to the aspect of who she is *beyond* her mind. Her being is hidden by who the mind tells her she is: her worries, concerns, fears, and judgments.

As the Eric Butterworth quote illustrates, we're often searching outside of ourselves for those deeper moments of peace. The relative world can provide moments of distraction that seem to pacify that yearning, yet these moments are never sustainable because we're living in a world of duality. I cannot know what the experience of pain is for example, if I haven't at some point experienced its opposite, pleasure. Consequently, on a daily basis, we experience one feeling and then its opposite. We vacillate between happiness and then sadness. Or desire and then fulfill-ment of that desire. Or frustration and calmness. And so it goes. All life experiences fall somewhere within this continuum of one feeling and its polar opposite.

As I explain to people who are curious, meditation is a way to shut out this relative world of opposites (if even for five minutes) and have an inner experience that transcends the continuum of emotional life experiences. After sitting in meditation, the per-son can feel the benefits of that inner experience throughout the day. Moments of peace, contentment, happiness, or love surge from within as opposed to being generated by outside circum-stances, generally reactive by nature: we scream at our lover, curse the landlord, berate ourselves for some incident. By simply taking a few minutes every day to check in, life can be dramati-cally transformed in a positive way. As we become more inter-nally referenced, we'll see ourselves more accurately as opposed to seeing ourselves through the eyes of how others falsely see us.

Lightening Up

Many people equate meditation with enlightenment. In my explaining meditation I want us to think of the word enlighten-ment in a different way. It means to be of light, to lighten up, to laugh, to not take day-to-day life experiences so seriously.

If you're a person who defines yourself primarily through the things you accomplish or the external gratification you receive (and who doesn't?), sometimes it's hard *not* to take your daily experiences so seriously. But when you begin to see that the process of going within naturally leads to lightening up because you're reconnecting to a part of yourself that isn't defined by outer circumstances (which are subject to change on a daily basis), then the idea of meditation doesn't seem to be so mystical.

I'm not asking you to go sit for years in a cold, dark cave somewhere in the most remote regions of India. Nor does having a moment of inner practice mean that who you are is going to lead you to becoming celibate. (No sex? Ever?) In your own process of "lightening up" you'll begin to have a new perspective on life and be liberated from your self-imposed drama. We're all major drama queens until we can glimpse a world that exists beyond our dramas.

What we're talking about here is that a major personal shift requires a move beyond the intellect to understand who we are. We can't reason our way to enlightenment. It's a process of opening our hearts. We can't reason our way to becoming more evolved or aware, more conscious. It doesn't happen through the mental faculty. It doesn't happen through reasoning. We need to stop thinking our way through life and start feeling our way through it instead.

". . . In Whoville They Say That The Grinch's Small Heart Grew Three Sizes That Day. . ."

When someone breaks up with us, it *does* feel as if our heart is breaking. Our brain doesn't feel devastated. When we're overjoyed it *feels* as if the heart is singing. The brain doesn't feel like belting the tune.

To "open our hearts" means approaching life's experiences from a heart-feeling space. Being with yourself and other people in a space of non-judgment, non-criticism, and without personal agendas; realizing when we judge and condemn others we're really judging and condemning the same behavior in ourselves. Although we will still meet certain people who might make it difficult to remain in that space. You know who they are: the one we call "a jerk" for not putting on his turn signal; the loud-mouthed drunk at the party; even the brother or sister who drives us crazy and pushes our buttons. The more we become aware, however, through patience and the cultivation of a meditation practice, we see some interesting things that weren't previously understandable to the ego mind. The more we exercise those qualities of the heart, the road to enlightenment — to opening up, to transformation — becomes an easier and navigable path. We see that there are other explanations besides the judgment that, "This jerk just cut me off." We consider other possibilities.

Maybe the guy was speeding because he just got news that his pregnant wife was giving birth and he's rushing to meet her. The loudmouth at the party? Perhaps he's drunk and heartbro-ken because his girlfriend just dumped him. The sister who gets on our nerves is perhaps the best teacher. She forces us to culti-vate characteristics of patience and forgiveness when it seems as if it would be so much easier to just wring her neck.

Being kind to yourself. Now that's a novel idea isn't it? The most important relationship or person in relationship with your-self is *you*. We're taught to believe that we're being selfish when we take time to do things for ourselves or put ourselves first. And yet how can we possibly show up in life, make a difference, contribute, and "be there" for anyone else if we first haven't been there for ourselves?

French philosopher, René Descartes, said, "I think, therefore I am." Descartes had it backwards. You *are* first. You are being, you are consciousness, which precedes thought. And because you *are,* you also have the ability to think. Actually you *are* whether you think or not.

We place too much emphasis on this thinking stuff. We've for-gotten the mind is one small aspect of our being. It's a part of our organism but not the whole. We falsely have identified ourselves with our thoughts and forgotten who we really are. And who we are has been clouded by the thoughts of who we think we are.

Infinite Blue Skies

Look at it this way. Let's pretend your natural being (who you truly are) is infinite blue sky. In your blueness you're having this beautiful day of blue. You're in "the zone," playing basketball, or hiking, singing in your car, dancing a ballet, or doing a scene in class where you're so in the moment that the experience becomes timeless. You're one with — or completely immersed in — your blueness. Suddenly this white puffy cloud comes rolling by and it says, "You're stupid." Then it passes.

You think, "Where did that come from?" but you forget about it and get lost again in your blue sky. You come back to your basketball game and then all of a sudden a few more clouds come rolling into your blueness: "You're ugly," "You're a loser," "You'll never amount to anything," "You're too old," "Who do you think you are?" and your clarity is, well, clouded.

Then a swarm of grey clouds move in and completely conceals your blueness from you. You become enveloped in grey. And for a moment — or longer — you forget about your blueness. Who wouldn't? All these other judgments and proclamations *seem* real. And you only believe what you can see, right? And since you can't see the blue anymore you believe in the grey. You become this violent cloud formation. You become these violent thoughts; they perpetuate false beliefs about yourself. "You're no good," "You're untalented," "You'll never amount to anything," *are* violent thoughts. They hide the truth of who you previously knew (or rather, experienced) yourself to be, before the clouds came in and obscured the authentic you.

What happens if we become an observer of these events and step outside of the experience? The sky is blue. We see grey clouds, so we don't see the blue anymore. We identify the grey as the color the sky presently appears. But it's not a grey sky. It's a blue sky that's been covered over by the grey clouds. Just because storm clouds form and the sky *appears* grey, doesn't mean that the sky *is* grey. It's not. The blueness may be concealed but it's still blue.

We've identified with these grey clouds to mean this is who I am; I am these thoughts. A lot of our time — days, months, years — are filled with forgetting (or not being able) to see the blue sky that's masked by the grey clouds. Part of the miracle of meditation is that, even if it's just for a nanosecond, we can peel back those grey clouds to have a glimpse of our own infinite blue. And the grey cloud cover may envelop us again but this brief connection to ourselves gives the awareness that we're not those things. Those negative thoughts are *not* who we are.

Meditation is a process in which we train ourselves to dwell in a space to reconnect with our blue sky. When we see beyond the grey clouds, we'll glimpse in meditation our inner truth. It's as vast as the bluest sky you've ever seen.

Homework, Week 15: Perhaps the best way to end our homework exercises is by taking a look at how often we let our lives escape us without our even realizing it. I discovered this exercise in *The Dance* by Oriah Mountain Dreamer. I was so struck by the simplicity and power of it that I've been using it to help artists ever since. Take three pieces of paper. On the top of page one, write: "What I Spend Time On." On the next page, write: "What I Spend Money On." On the last page, write: "What I Spend Energy On." Now start writing.

Write whatever comes to mind. What do you spend time on? Work? Going to the gym? Worrying? Paying bills? Don't edit yourself. Keep writing. Do you spend time fighting? Making love? Getting angry? Partying?

The goal of the exercise is to not judge yourself for doing any of these things, but to write them down. After you've written at least a page worth, move on to the next category. Ask the same question about money and start writing. What do you spend it on? Food? Clothes? Other people? A good book? Just write whatever comes to mind. Then, when you are finished, move on to the last category. What do you spend energy on? What is it? Lying? Pretending? Being fearful? Giving? Taking trips? There are no wrong answers.

After you have completed all three pages look at your lists. Compare them. See what you find. Be kind to yourself. Maybe some things will surprise you that you didn't know you were spending a lot of anything on. Once you have reviewed your list, ask yourself this question: "With the limited amount of time I've been given on this planet, why would I want to spend any more time, energy or money on things that neither bring me value or make me happy? Things that make me unfulfilled or sad? Things that make me feel disconnected and scattered? Things that hurt? These are good questions to ask. Maybe you really need to re-examine the things on which you're spending energy.

Go back to the three lists. Circle three (just three) things from each list that bring you the most joy, the most fun in your life. There's probably more, but let's stick with that number. So, when complete you will have circled a total of nine activities or actions.

Look at your lists and put an "X" through three things from each of the categories that bring you the most unhappiness and distress. When done, you should have a total of nine "X"s. Now go back one more time to both lists. From the circled list of nine, choose *three* that are most fulfilling and write them on a new sheet of paper. Then look at the "X" list of nine, and choose *three* that bring you the most dissatisfaction or are a complete waste. Write them on the new sheet of paper.

The final homework: spend more time on the three activities you circled that you enjoy the most. If it's sailing, go do it. If it's meditating, go do it. Then take the three you put an "X" through and eliminate completely for the week. *What?* Yes. Give up worrying for a week. Yes. Give up gossiping for a week. Yes. Give up eating junk food for a week. Spend more time doing what brings you joy and less time doing things that make you feel crappy. Our lives on this planet are short. Maybe the realization is to no longer waste giving energy to those things that are spiritually, emotionally and even physically shortening it even more.

Keep away from people who belittle your ambitions. Small people always do that. But the really great make you feel that you, too, can become great."

— Mark Twain

PARTING IS SUCH SWEET SORROW

"Let no one come to you without leaving better and happier."
— Mother Teresa

"Our deepest fear is not that we are inadequate. Our deepest fear is that we are powerful beyond measure. It is our light, not our darkness that most frightens us. We ask ourselves, 'Who am I to be brilliant, gorgeous, talented, fabulous?' Actually, who are you not to be? You are a child of God. Your playing small does not serve the world. There is nothing enlightened about shrinking so that other people won't feel insecure around you. We are all meant to shine, as children do. We were born to make manifest the glory of God that is within us. It is not just in some of us; it is in everyone. And as we let our own light shine, we unconsciously give other people permission to do the same. As we are liberated from our own fear, our presence automatically liberates others."
— **Marianne Williamson**

These beautiful words seem to me a benediction, a spiritual call-to-arms, in how to live one's life. Whenever I personally forget that living this way is possible — living at cause, being able to make a difference through my art, interacting with others from a place of authentic being, aligning with the truth (not the conditioned thoughts) of who I am — this quote reaffirms and reminds me that not only is anything possible but to *not* live and create from this truth is a sacrilege to myself. To the potential of being human. To the spark of my infinite creativity wishing to be expressed.

As artists, it's important we don't lose sight of that hope, that possibility, that miracle which resides within each of us. It's this fundamental truth that keeps us going, and inspires us when all else seems to be failing. Ms. Williamson's stirring words are a reminder that living our lives and creating our art from any place other than the truth of who we *are* is really a life not lived.

But, of course, we already know this. We've known this since the very beginning.

So if you were absolutely sure about this what would you do? Today. Right now. Let your hair down and your spirit fly. Live your life gloriously. Stop apologizing for yourself and your existence. You are the only *you* ever created since the beginning of time. You deserve to be here. It's staggering to realize this. From since the earth was born some 4.5 billion years ago all the way into perpetuity, there will never be another *you.*

Ever.

So beat your drum. Sing your song. Write your story. Stand up and own this tiny sliver of this mere blip of this infinitesimal and yet extraordinary and miraculous thing called your existence. You are here now. You never will be again. What an amazing confluence of events that had to occur to give birth to your existence in this moment.

Live the grandness of that truth.

Because it's certainly epic.

Just like you.

REFERENCES

[1] "Pablo Picasso." Quotes.net. STANDS4 LLC, 2011. 15 September. 2011. http://www.quotes.net/quote/3662

[2] **Carlos Castaneda.** *The Teachings of Don Juan: A Yaqui Way of Knowledge, University of California Press, 1969.*

[3] **The Essential Rumi**, *translated by Coleman Barks, Quality Paperback Book Club, 1995.*

[4] "**American Life**," *from **American Life**, written by Mirwais Ahmadzi & Madonna Louise Ciccone, EMI Music Publishing, Warner/ Chappell Music, Inc., 22nd April 2003.*

[5] **Brené Brown.** "The Power of Vulnerability.", TED Houston, Houston, TX. June 2010. In Person. http://www.ted.com/talks/ brene_brown_on_vulnerability.html   .

[6] **Joseph Campbell.** *The Power of Myth, with Bill Moyers, Anchor Books, 1988.*

[7] **Steve Jobs.** "Commencement Address." Stanford Graduation Address. University of Stanford. Graduation, Sanford, CA. June12, 2005. In Person.

[8] **Hugh Elliott,** *Standing Room Only weblog, 02-14-2003* Author of the *Standing Room Only Weblog (http://www.blogs.salon. com/0001573).*

[9] **Robert Duvall.** *An interview with Robert Duvall, NPR: All Things Considered, "Still Living In The Potential," June 1st, 2010.*

[10] **Ben Brantley.** *"Home Is Where The Soul Aches", The New York Times, February 19th, 2010.*

[11] "Richard Buckminster Fuller." Quotes.net. STANDS4 LLC, 2011. 15 September. 2011. http://www.quotes.net/quote/7378

[12] "Thomas Huxley." Quotes.net. STANDS4 LLC, 2011. 15 September. 2011. http://www.quotes.net/quote/1542

[13] Janeane Garofalo. *Standup Performance*, Date Unknown.

[14] Cal Fussman. *"What I've Learned: Christopher Reeve Superhero, 51, Bedford, New York."* Interview. *Esquire* Dec.-Jan. 2003: Print.

[15] *Webster's New World Dictionary, The World Publishing Company, 1968.*

[16] Ferguson, Marilyn. *The Aquarian Conspiracy: Personal and Social Transformation in Our Time. Los Angeles: J. P. Tarcher/ Houghton Mifflin, 1987.*

[17] Tolle, Eckhart (2004). *The Power of Now (2004 edition).* New World Library and Namaste Publishing. p. xv

[18] *Kate Bush. "Running Up That Hill," from Hounds of Love, EMI Music Publishing, 1997.*

[19] Charles Reade. *Notes and Queries* (9th Series), attributed to, Volume 12, 17th October, 1903.

[20] Unknown Source, attributed to Roger Ebert, film critic.

[21] Unknown Source, attributed to Ralph Waldo Emerson.

[22] K. H. Pribram. Holonomic brain theory, New Trends in Experimental & Clinical Psychiatry, Vol 5(1), Jan-Mar 1989, 53-78.

[23] Barbara Stoler Miller. *The Bhagavad-Gita, translated by, Quality Paperback Book Club, 1986, pp. 46.*

[24] Hermes Trismegistus. The Emerald Tablet Of Hermes, CreateSpace (August 16, 2011)

25 **Guatama Buddha**. *Dhammapada : a collection of verses from the Pali Canon of Buddhism translated from the pali* by F. Max Muller. St Petersburg, Fla: Red and Black Publishers, 2008.

26 **Albert Einstein**. *Einstein For Beginners*, Joseph Schwartz & Michael McGuinness, Pantheon Books, New York, 1979. pp. 169

27 *Avatar*. Dir. James Cameron. Perf. Zoe Saldana & Sam Worthington. 20th Century Fox, 2009. DVD.

28 **Bryson, Bill**. *A Short History of Nearly Everything*, New York: Broadway Books, 2003.

29 **Lanza, Robert**. *"A New Theory of the Universe: Biocentrism Builds on Quantum Physics by Putting Life into the Equation."* American Scholar 22 Mar. 2007: n. pg. Print.

31 **"Rainer Maria Rilke."** BrainyQuote.com. Xplore Inc, 2011. 18 September. 2011. http://www.brainyquote.com/quotes/authors/r/rainer_maria_rilke.html

32 **Throeau, Henry David**. Quotes. N.d. (1817–1862) American writer & philosopher.

33 **"Albert Schweitzer."** Quotes.net. STANDS4 LLC, 2011. 18 September. 2011. http://www.quotes.net/quote/4097

34 **Knight, Christopher**. *"Sarah Palin Trashes National Endowment for the Arts."* Web log post. *Culture Monster*. LA Times, 16 Mar. 2011. Web. 18 Sept. 2011. http://latimesblogs.latimes.com/culturemonster/2011/03/palin-trashes-national-endowment-for-the-arts.html   .

35 **Osho**, *Creativity: Unleashing the Forces Within*, St. Martin's Griffin, 1999, pp. 91, 97, pp. 64

36 **King, Susan**. *"Classic Hollywood: Rita Moreno Reflects on 'quite a Life'"* LA Times 27 June 2011: n. pag. Print.

[37] **Byron, David.** *"How Does Your Garden Grow?"* *Theatre Communications Group*. TCG, Jan. 2005. Web. 18 Sept. 2011. <http://www.tcg.org/publications/at/jan05/roundtable.cfm>.

[38] **Margo Jefferson** *"Memo to Actors: Learn to Master The Essentials"*, *The New York Times*.

[39] **De, Mille Agnes.**"The War." *Martha: the Life and Work of Martha Graham*. New York: Random House, 1991. P.264. Print.

[40] **Cole, Kenneth.** "Today Is Not a Dress Rehearsal." *Breaking News and Opinion*. Huffington Post, 18 Jan. 2009. Web. 18 Sept. 2011. http://www.huffingtonpost.com/kenneth-cole/today-is-not-a-dress-rehe_b_158781.html.

[41] **Carnegie, Dale.** "Daily Dose of Confidence Blog." *Corporate Training, Leadership Training, and Sales Training*. Dale Carnegie Training®, 19 May 2009. Web. 18 Sept. 2011.

<http://blog.dalecarnegie.com/daily-dose-of-confidence/daily-dose-of-confidence-519/>.

[42] **Joseph Campbell.** "Freidrich Von Schiller Quote (1759-1804)" *The Power of Myth* w. Bill Moyers Ed. Betty Sue Flowers, Doubleday, 1988, pp. 4.

[43] **Jong, Erica.** *Becoming Light: Poems, New and Selected*. New York, NY: Harper Perennial, 1992. Print.

[44] **Cummings, E. E.** *Love Is a Place*. New York: Koco NY, 1994. Print.

[45] **Ram Dass.** *Paths to God: Living the Bhagavad Gita*, Harmony Books, 2004. pp. 69-70.

[46] **Osho.** *Intuition: Knowing Beyond Logic*, St. Martin's Griffin, 2001, pp. xiii.

[47] **Hiscock, John.** *"Wanted: Johnny Depp"* Thestar.com. *News, Toronto, GTA, Sports, Business, Entertainment, Canada, World,*

Breaking. The Star, 27 June 2009. Web. 18 Sept. 2011. <http://www.thestar.com/article/656760>.

[48] **Alan Cummings**, An interview with *Backstage West,* date unknown

49 **Ryan Gosling.** *"Drive Interview: Ryan Gosling Is in the Driver's Seat."* Interview by Joel D. Amos. *Movie Fanatic.* N.p., Sept. 2011. Web. 18 Sept. 2011. http://www.moviefanatic.com/2011/09/drive-interview-ryan-gosling-is-in-the-drivers-seat/.

[50] **Brice, Fanny.** As quoted in *Words of Wisdom : More Good Advice* (1990) by William Safire and Leonard Safir, p. 185

[51] **Gaga, Lady.** "Don't You Ever Let a Soul in the World Tell You That You Can't Be Exactly Who You Are." Web log comment. *Twitter.* N.p., n.d. Web. 19 Sept. 2011. http://twitter.com/LadyGaga.

[52] **Hinz Evelyn J.** *D. H. Lawrence: An Unprofessional Study* (1932); also quoted in *The Mirror and the Garden : Realism and Reality in the Writings of Anais Nin* (1971), p. 40

[53] **Lanza, R.** *Biocentrism : How Life and Consciousness are the Keys to Understanding the True Nature of the Universe.* Dallas, TX Jackson, TN: BenBella Books, Inc. Distributed by Perseus Distribution, 2009, pp.99

[54] **Frank, Adam.** "Time Is Constant, But How We Perceive It Varies." Interview. *Talk of The Nation.* National Public Radio. WNPR, CT, 23 June 2011. Radio. Transcript.

[55] **Deepak Chopra.** *The Seven Spiritual Laws of Success*, Amber-Allen Publishing, 1994, pp. 73.

[56] **Keller, Helen.** *The Open Door.* Garden City, NY: Doubleday, 1957. Print.

[57] **Agnes De Mille.** Interviewed by Howard, Jane. "The Grand Dame of Dance." *Life Magazine* 15 Nov. 1963: 89-94. Print.

[58] **Meryl Streep.** *"Veteran Play: Thirty years ago Meryl and Al met cute now they meet nasty (on screen) for the first time ever in Tony Kushner's epic* Angels in America,*"* Entertainment Weekly, December 5, 2003.

[59] **Abraham H. Maslow,** *The Further Reaches of Human Nature,* (New York: The Viking Press, 1971) (New York: Penquin Books, 1976; Arkana, 1993).

[60] "Sandra Bullock Oscar Interview." Interview by Charlie Rose. *Charlie Rose Show.* 10 Feb. 2010. Television.

[61] **W.H. Murray;** foreword by Hamish MacInnes. *The Evidence of Things Not Seen: A Mountaineer's Tale* an autobiography. City: Baton Wicks Publications, 2002.

[62] "Jerry Lewis Quotes." *Quotations.* Date unknown.

[63] **Pennington, Bill.** "Hitched to Miller, U.S. Skiing Slips Off Course - New York Times." *The New York Times - Breaking News, World News & Multimedia.* N.p., 19 Feb. 2006. Web. 20 Sept. 2011. <http://www.nytimes.com/2006/02/19/sports/olympics/19bode.html?pagewanted=print>.

[64] **Jim Carrey,** *The Reader's Digest, March, 2006, p. 81.*

[65] **Todd London.** *"Andre Gregory Sees the Light"*, American Theatre Magazine, March, 2005, pp. 50-51.

[66] **Watts, Naomi.** "For Anyone Who Ever Needed A Reminder For What Can Happen When You Hold onto Your Dreams, Here She Is." Interview by Ingrid Sischy. *LynchNet: The David Lynch Resource.* N.p., Dec. 2003. Web. 20 Sept. 2011. <http://www.lynchnet.com/mdrive/wattsint.html>.

[67] Dustin Hoffman *"Quotations."* Date unknown.

[68] "John Lennon." 1-Famous-Quotes.com. Gledhill Enterprises, 2011.

Tue Sep 20 01:03:27 2011. http://www.1-famous-quotes.com/quote/1180865.

[69] **Winfrey, Oprah.** "What Oprah Knows for Sure About Finding Success - Oprah.com." Editorial. *O. The Oprah Magazine* Sept. 2001: n. pag. Print.

[70] **Albert Einstein.** As quoted in *Journal of France and Germany* (1942 - 1944) by Gilbert Fowler White, in excerpt published in *Living with Nature's Extremes : The Life of Gilbert Fowler White* (2006) by Robert E. Hinshaw, p. 62.

[71] **Craig Hamilton** An interview with Amit Goswami *"Scientific Proof of the Existence of God,"* from *What is Enlightenment?* Magazine, Issue 11, Spring-Summer, 1997. From his book *The Self-Aware Universe: How Consciousness Creates the Material World.*

[72] **Lanza, R.** *Biocentrism : How Life and Consciousness are the Keys to Understanding the True Nature of the Universe.* Dallas, TX Jackson, TN: BenBella Books, Inc. Distributed by Perseus Distribution, 2009, pp.55.

[73] **Joseph Campbell.** *The Power of Myth,* Doubleday, 1988. pp. 160-161.

[74] **Ram Dass.** Swami Brahmananda quote from *Journey Of Awakening: A Meditator's Guidebook* 1978, pp. 20.

[75] **Marianne Williamson,** *The Gift of Change: Spiritual Guidance for a Radically New Life,* Harper San Francisco, 2004, pp. 88.

[76] **Williams, Tennessee.** Camino Real. New York: New Directions, 1970.

[77] "Erich Fromm." 1-Famous-Quotes.com. Gledhill Enterprises, 2011.

Tue Sep 20 01:24:59 2011. http://www.1-famous-quotes.com/quote/178235.

[78] Taylor, Jill Bolte. *My Stroke of Insight: a Brain Scientist's Personal Journey*. New York: Viking, 2008. Print.

[79] **Cameron James.** Address to the 2010 TED .conference (13 February 2010).

[80] **The Buddha.** Date unknown

[81] **Nietzsche, Friedrich Wilhelm,** Anthony Mario Ludovici, and J. M. Kennedy. *The Case of Wagner.* New York: Macmillan, 1924. Print. Pg. 56.

[82] *The Essential Rumi* (1995) translated by Coleman Barks with John Moyne, A. J. Arberry and Reynold Nicholson "On Gambling" Ch. 18 : The Three Fish, p. 193.

[83] **Butterworth, Eric.** *Discover the Power Within You: a Guide to the Unexplored Depths Within.* City: HarperOne, 2008.

[84] **Twain, Mark.** *"Quotations", US humorist, novelist, short story author, & wit (1835 - 1910).*

[85] **Mother Teresa.** As quoted in *Worldwide Laws of Life : 200 Eternal Spiritual Principles* (1998) by John Templeton, p. 448.

[86] **Williamson, Marianne.** (1996). *A Return to Love: Reflections on the Principles of A Course in Miracles.* New York: HarperCollins. 1992. From Chapter 7, Section 3.

ADDITIONAL READING

To further help you on your meditative/creative journey, I suggest reading some of these books by these authors:

Ram Dass: *The Journey of Awakening: A Mediators Guidebook* or *Be Here Now*

http://www.ramdass.org/

Jon Kabat-Zinn: *Wherever You Go, There You Are*

http://www.mindfulnesstapes.com/

Osho: anything of his (he will blow your mind!)

http://www.osho.com/

Deepak Chopra: same goes for him!

http://deepakchopra.com/

http://www.chopra.com/

Henry David Thoreau: old school, but classic and still so relevant, especially *Walden* or *Life in the Woods*

http://www.walden.org/

Marianne Williamson: *A Return to Love*

http://www.marianne.com/

Rainer Maria Rilke's *Letters to a Young Poet*

Eckhart Tolle: *The Power of Now*

http://www.eckharttolle.com/

Anne Lamott: *Bird by Bird*

Louise Hay: *You Can Heal Your Life* and other books by her

http://www.louisehay.com/

Esther and Jerry Hicks: *The Law of Attraction, Ask and It Is Given, The Astonishing Power of Emotions*

http://www.abraham-hicks.com/lawofattractionsource/index.php

Steven Pressfield, *The War Of Art,* will help you overcome your resistance to creating

http://www.stevenpressfield.com/

Paramahansa Yogananda: too many to list here

http://www.yogananda-srf.org/

David Mamet – *True & False: Heresy And Common Sense For The Actor*

Tony Robbins – www.tonyrobbins.com

And there are so many others who have inspired me along the way, I can't list them all. These people, and so many more, have inspired and influenced my work greatly. I would have no book would it not be for their collective teachings.

ABOUT THE AUTHOR

Anthony Meindl is an award-winning writer, producer, director and actor. As Artistic Director of Anthony Meindl's Actor Workshop (AMAW) in Los Angeles – where the "right brain rules" - he is endlessly inspired by his student's fearless creativity. Mr. Meindl's first feature screenplay, THE WONDER GIRLS, was the Grand Prize Winning Feature Screenplay in the Slamdance Film Festival Screenplay Competition in 2007. The film is slated for production in 2012 in Berlin.

Meindl's other credits include the award-winning 35-mm short film, READY? OK! and the feature film BIRDS OF A FEATHER (with Olympia Dukakis, Bruce Vilanch, Trevor Donovan and Lindsay Hollister and is currently in post-production); both of which he wrote, directed, and produced. AT LEFT BRAIN TURN RIGHT is his first book.

Made in the USA
San Bernardino, CA
24 June 2018